"Well done! a superb labour of love. A nice b
of good humour, sound advice and the disti]

PETER HARRISON PhD, Senior Research Fellow,
Oceans, National Research Council Canada

"A great read, a perceptive contribution to what our employees need to read and digest. I am anxious to pass the book on and listen to the chortling and giggling come from someone else's office for a while."

STEVE BLACKWELL, Manager
Knowledge Coordination, Prairie & Northern Region, Environment Canada

"Read your book and enjoyed it immensely. Look forward to offering it to my managers and staff."

R. JIM CLARK, Director
Compliance Verification, Customs, Prairie Region

"I really enjoyed the chapter on mentors. You provide good advice, which I know I am going to take. Your stories from your own life add a welcome personal touch. It is as if the reader is actually listening to the words of his/her mentor, gaining helpful advice and learning life lessons."

MELANIE MATIAS (Intern)
Immigration and Refugee Board, Prairie Region

"My son is thinking of a public service career and I will recommend your book to him as a thought-provoking read for anyone contemplating such a career."

SCOTT SERSON, President (retired)
Public Service Commission of Canada

" I would like to see this book being used as part of an orientation initiative in our management training and in specific departments and agencies. ... I might also suggest that this book could be read by people on the other side of the spectrum—those ready to retire—so they too may become motivated to tell their stories and help sustain the importance of the public service."

JAMES KENDRICK PhD, Director General
Social Development Canada

" I am new to the public service. A lot of things rang true...especially the chapters on busyness and time! ...people who have been around for years forget what it was like when they started...your book should be handed to every public servant when they sign their letter of offer..."

SHARI EISLER

"...full of practical nuggets for young public servants...a really good book—wish I had something like it when I was a young public servant."

JANICE COCHRANE, President
Canada School of Public Service

"...it articulates other thoughts I've had, like how fulfilling it is working for something other than the bottom line. Good work! I definitely think this can help us kids sort ourselves out and make a difference in the public service. Thanks for writing these letters. I have been waiting. Good leader!

CHRISTINE KALLIKRAGAS, Claims Analyst
Yukon Regional Office, Indian & Northern Affairs Canada

"This book is a must-read for those new to the public service. It delves into the root values inherent in the words 'service to the public' and clearly articulates what it means to be a public servant; not often stated in the 'rah rah' private sector focus of today's governments. At the same time it provides critical and reflective thinking for contemporary public service managers."

ANNE SCHULTZ, Director (retired)
Master of Arts in Leadership and Training, Royal Roads University

Bureaucratically Incorrect

Published by Doghouse Publishing
Second Impression 2005

#5 – 2318, 17th Street S.E.,
Calgary, Alberta
CANADA T2G 5R5
e-mail: chartb@telus.net
Phone: (403) 264•2919 / Fax: (403) 221•3079

National Library of Canada Cataloguing in Publication

Chartier, Bob 1947–
Bureaucratically incorrect: letters to a young public servant / Bob Chartier

Includes bibliographical references.
    ISBN 0–9733985–0–7

    1. Civil service—Canada. I. Title.

HD8013.C34C43 2004   352.6'3'0971   C2004-900655-X

EDITING: Pam Withers and Jeremy Drought
COVER, INTERIOR DESIGN AND PRODUCTION: Jeremy Drought, *Last Impression Publishing Service*, Calgary, Alberta
COVER IMAGE: *Boss with Staff* / A47C71 / Brand X Pictures / Alamy Ltd.
PROOFREADING: Rod McPherson and Frank Osendarp
PHOTO OF AUTHOR: Jeremy Drought, *Last Impression Publishing Service*, Calgary, Alberta. Bob is standing in front of a painting entitled *Night Canopy* by Linda Littler-Chartier.
Printed and bound in Canada by *Houghton Boston*, Saskatoon, Saskatchewan

Hell, there are no rules here—
we're trying to accomplish something.

Thomas Alva Edison

Bureaucratically Incorrect

Letters to a Young Public Servant

BOB CHARTIER

DOGHOUSE PUBLISHING

About this Book

THERE ARE MORE THAN 2.8 MILLION PUBLIC SERVANTS IN CANADA. They teach our kids, protect our borders, safeguard our environment and so much more. To choose a career in public service is to choose to make a difference rather than a profit. It is an important distinction and a choice for those who make it-often saddled with less respect and a greater scrutiny attached to it than most would have anticipated.

Bureaucratically Incorrect: Letters to a Young Public Servant is the latest in a series of personal initiatives that collectively represent my commitment to improving both the perceptions and experiences of Canadian public service-the former for citizens served; the later for those who work within it. Presented as a series of letters or monologues from an aging public servant to new recruits and younger employees who have many years of service ahead of them in which they can still make a difference, Bureaucratically Incorrect presents some ideas on key issues and areas of concern like History, Citizens, Governance, Learning, Teamwork, Technology, Leadership, Communication, Change, Innovation, Manners, Rewards, Ethics, Busyness, Words, Space, Diversity, Practice, Time, Rights and Mentors.

Discussion, thoughtful action and a commitment to the evolution of these ideas will always be necessary if we are to succeed in keeping public service on a cutting edge of the best in leadership and people management, technological and scientific innovations and improved service to our citizens.

Bureaucratically Incorrect may infuriate and provoke criticism from some quarters and certainly it may be judged as controversial. Nevertheless, my hope is that the book will encourage a lively and constructive debate among those who work in public service, and the focus of any debate will always be in the spirit of service improvements that build pride in those of us who have chosen to do the work and respect from those for whom we toil.

Dedication

THIS BOOK IS DEDICATED WITH LOVE TO MY FAMILY especially Linda, my daughters Leah and Lark, who already show public service spirit and for Rob who, if given the chance, would have bested me at both public service and writing.

Acknowledgments

I WOULD LIKE TO ACKNOWLEDGE THE SUPPORT AND ENCOURAGEMENT I've received over the years from risk-taking executives who created a space for my work to flourish. Senior leaders such as Scott Serson, Peter Harrison, Janice Cochran, Jocelyn Bourgon, Garry Wouters, Wayne Wouters, Mel Cappe, Caroline Davis, Gordon Shanks and especially to the memory of Michael Nurse, a straight ahead public service executive whose support and great style helped create a space for this work.

Front line leaders such as John Watson, Sandy Thomson, Richard Rochefort, Adele Colby, Barb Martin, Paulette Panzeri and Claudette Pepper gave me both ground support and good counsel.

Colleagues in the workplace like Karen Bonner, Paul Lefebvre, Jill Lang Ward and Sylvie Lapointe have all helped me develop a greater vision.

Lee Rome, Joe Schaffer, Iryna Reim, Ed McKenzie, Anne Shultz, Graham Dixon and Monique Cikaliuk — my faculty colleagues at Royal Roads University gave me the opportunity to rediscover my love for teaching.

Bob Kennedy (Tehaliwaskenhas), Frank Osendarp and Bruce Anderson are the sort of friends who never let me rest on my ideas and whose gentle critiques helped form my thinking.

I am indebted to Pam Withers and Rod McPherson for their editorial assistance with early drafts of the manuscript and especially lucky to find Jeremy Drought whose eye and experience are responsible for the final edit as well as the design and production of the book.

Finally, thank you to all the young public servants that have responded to this work and helped me to confirm that the return on investment in public sector organizations is centered on the way we work with the next generation.

Bob Chartier
Calgary, Alberta

CAVEAT

The opinions expressed in this book are solely those of the author
and not (as yet) those of his employers.

Contents

Preface

THIS LITTLE BOOK HAS BEEN TRYING TO REACH YOU FOR MANY YEARS. I am a voracious reader but a tentative writer. I am a free thinker and a public servant. I am also a teacher and a life-long learner.

As such, I have always experienced a measure of frustration when I visit my local bookstore — looking for something new from which to learn. While I can always find dozens of new books on leadership, learning, change and so on, all of them are written with the private sector in mind. When I look harder for any similar books directed at those of my genus, the working public servant, they don't exactly jump off the shelves.

I have often reflected upon my early years in the public service. What I would have given — back then — to find a book written by a "graybeard," that would have given me some insight into what I had signed up for.

I will not make any advance claims over the value this book may hold for you. The passage of time and feedback from readers will tell me soon enough.

My claim is that I have given the writing of such a book as this a fair shot. A desire for honesty, brevity and common sense has guided my writing. It is neither a business book nor an academic tome. I feel I owe a debt of inspiration to both Rainier Maria Rilke who wrote *Letters to a Young Poet* in 1903 and, more recently, to Christopher Hitchens, the author of *Letters to a Young Contrarian.*

As I wrote my *Letters to a Young Public Servant*, I imagined I could see each of my intended readers and I tried to talk directly to you. You know who you are. You are the young men and women I have met across this huge wonderful country, who work within one or another of the diverse federal, provincial, municipal and First Nations public services. As this book goes to press, it is once again an opportune time to reflect on the role of public service in our society.

Bureaucratically incorrect

In Canada we have been pummeled with a score of near plague like scenarios in the past few years. We have been hit with hurricanes on the east coast, SARS in the cities, floods in Quebec, drought, West Nile virus, a mad cow on the prairies and wildfires in the west. We recall the real tension in the voices of nurses in great personal danger on the wards, yet they never hesitated in their commitment to sick Canadians. Public servants are always on the front line when things go horribly wrong. They are also there it seems, when government and contractors just go wrong on the front page of *The Globe and Mail*.

The fallout from the Auditor General's Report and other investigative reports from the provinces around alleged misuse of taxpayer dollars often point the first finger at public servants. Public servants work in a constantly shifting space between the democratic certainty of the elected Minister and the demands and needs of the citizens we serve. We cannot diminish the importance of one for the other. We serve Ministers first but we must remain true to our ethical standards. The question of whistle blowing has become an ongoing conversation in columns of newsprint, corridors of power and cubicles of insecurity. Public servants understand that they are often more front and center than most workers in the social order and there are pressures and ideologies that would willingly diminish the value of their work.

Compare the contribution of the private and public sectors in areas of public health, fire management and flood rescue and we do very well. One may also argue that there are public servants who could also match their private sector counterparts in communication, training and leadership skills. More to the point, we could do it for far less taxpayer dollars than some of the contractor rates we see alleged in our national newspapers.

Shortly after September 11, 2001 when I wrote this article for *Macleans* magazine, I had been thinking about those of us — young and old — who work in the public sector.

Over the thirty years that I have been a public servant, there have been more times than I would care to admit when I would not have been very comfortable disclosing that fact in conversation, much less declaring it in print. That I do so now is because I know we will need many young Canadians to choose a career with the public service in the next few years.

I will further disclose that in more recent years — as I suspect it has been for everyone else in public service — my world has been rocked; one cornerstone of my worldview is the international community of public service.

Thus, the embassy bombings, the federal building in Oklahoma City, and the September 11 airline attack on the World Trade Center and the Pentagon — all these events bring back images of public servants running towards the horror, instead of away from it; images that will stay with us forever. I have recognized and reconciled the fact that in many a terrorist's mind, foreign governments — the offices and buildings of administrations or regimes they don't agree with — have become their targets and, as we know, public servants are the front-line of governance.

For years, public servants have struggled with what I will describe as a "poor cousin" image in the workplace. It has long been insinuated that the brightest and the best were destined for employment in the private sector that they might shine ever brighter, live faster, move and shake and, of course, make the big bucks. The rest of us, for myriad reasons, make the decision to spend our working lives teaching your kids, hooking up your intravenous, protecting your border, checking the maintenance record on the aircraft taking you to Cancun, and responding to 911 calls…

We did hear some of your snickers over the years.

We heard your comments on road crews leaning on their shovels, on striking nurses, mindless clerks processing paper, lazy teachers and cops in doughnut shops. This was the tame stuff. There are also some really scary people out there who hate us. I believe it's time to re-think our views on public service. First of all, understand that we do a lot of things that no one else really wants to do…and there is no real money in it. I'm thinking; try to buy police services from a street vendor. Look on the open market for a qualified scientist to test your daughter's prescription drugs that will ensure your new grandchild is healthy and complete. What price would the market pay to find an illegal immigrant? Ask a major private-sector company to write a new fair-trade policy. Shop around for a good deal on a passport.

The private enterprise, capitalist system is fine by me. It is adept at doing those things it is supposed to do, but it can't do it all. When it comes to writing good policy on parole violation, we don't place the contract up for tender; we ask a public servant with a scholar's background, a wealth of experience and an awareness of the word on the street. When we need protection, or high standards in our goods, food and water, we again look to the public servant.

Whoops, let's stop right there for a moment. On that water thing, you are right; we have Walkerton and North Battleford to consider. I grew up in North Battleford. For decades, I've known that public service employees drew drinking water a kilometer downstream from the spot in the river where sewage was dumped. I was appalled and, as a working government guy myself, embarrassed and a shamed.

Let's be honest. Public servants make mistakes — big ones, little ones, and some really stupid ones. But so does the private sector. Our trouble, as public servants, is that our mistakes can cause a lot more grief to a lot more people than someone who forgets to add the service charges to that SUV lease contract at the local car dealership.

It is true, that we have been notorious for our red tape, our obsession with paper and our lack of efficiency from time to time, but please be assured; we are working really hard to improve on all these issues. We can and will become as fast, effective and quality-minded as the private sector, perhaps more so. However, we have many masters, and sometimes when we try to cut the red tape, eliminate the paperwork and speed things up, we get beaten up for what is then framed as a lack of accountability. It's often difficult for us to know whom we really serve — politicians or citizens. I believe we can serve both and do so without compromising accountability or effectiveness.

So what have public service employees got here?

Well, we have a job that has little or no market value. We have employment that is under constant public scrutiny. We get paid whatever citizens — not what the market — thinks we are worth, and we provide always essential but often hidden services.

And did you know most of us really enjoy our work! We love your kids that we teach, we feel for you in the intensive care unit, we want to find the bad guys and we are driven to develop policy that reflects Canadian values. We are called to service as we work with the homeless and the unfortunate, despite the fact there is not a great deal of monetary reward or even significant prestige associated with the work.

Nowadays, more than ever before, I suppose, public servants may feel like they are the target for evil and just plain meanness, but they will go to work every day and they will be there for us, running first towards the trouble, and leading the rebuilding. The war on terrorism will not be fought in the private sector; rather it will be defended at the border, through policy-making decisions on privacy and in the day-to-day readiness of emergency services workers.

So, if I have never said it to you before, let me thank you for giving me this work, and letting me do it for you.

The article still stands for me...for you as well, I trust.

Introduction

WHEN ONE IS MAKING A CHOICE ABOUT A CAREER, the clearest line in the sand is that which differentiates the public from the private sector. Review the following list: These are just a few of the issues with which public-sector employees will be confronted and expected to work on/resolve over the next decade.

- Literacy and education for children around the world
- Maintenance and development of the national health-care system; infant mortality, public health
- Space exploration
- Declining marine fish populations
- Threats and costs to public health and safety caused by obesity, tobacco, alcohol and drug addiction
- Research and development of alternative sources of energy: fuel cells, wind, solar and tidal
- International terrorism — intelligence, discovery, location, control; increased security and restrictions on travel
- Civil rights, freedom of speech, expression, privacy, geographical movement
- Climatic change: rising temperatures, receding glaciers, falling water tables, encroaching deserts
- Weapons proliferation and gun control
- Unadulterated sources/supplies of food and water
- Protection/preservation of natural and historic sites, monuments, cultural artefacts, treasures and antiquities
- More and better public transportation

- Rising public cost of (and response to) the increased incidence of mental health issues, violence and homelessness
- Garbage and toxic waste control and clean-up
- National and international monetary controls, interest rate stabilization and the fairness of income tax systems
- GM (genetically modified) research on food, babies and law enforcement
- Land-use policy, agriculture and environmental protection – water and air quality, soil erosion, deforestation, ocean pollution, loss of habitat and species extinction
- AIDS, SARS, BSE, West Nile, and the next plague
- Increasing life expectancy and elder care in an aging population
- Research, ethical testing and marketing of safe pharmaceuticals
- Improving our collective response to racism and religious intolerance
- Quality of life issues — health and safety in the workplace; life-long, continuing education and research
- Military and civil defence and security
- Global population movement and control, immigration and emigration – its effects on health and prosperity
- Emergency health, rescue and disaster services

Or you could opt for a job in the private sector, designing a bigger and more attractive sports utility vehicle. Okay, perhaps that is not entirely fair. After all, the private sector is the "economic engine" that enables nations and the whole world to keep going round, and a free market economy ensures goods and services are delivered — hopefully — on the basis of supply and demand.

Trouble is, certain critical supplies are running a little low these days and demand is often based more on want than need.

These few public policy issues I have listed are indeed writ large and involve thousands of smaller issues and problems. They all invite the creation of data and documents and the opening up millions of files, folders and portfolios. Within each and every public sector file there will also be a significant role for the private sector. Drug companies invest in science,

Bureaucratically Incorrect

make drugs and turn a profit. Governments, as regulators, make sure the drugs don't kill us. It's a good balance.

Shell Oil will probably lead the way in the development of a hydrogen cell engine. Trouble is, we almost had to see an end to oil reserves before they got started. Private-sector energy and public-sector caution are so often at their best after the horse has thrown the rider.

Let's take one of these public policy issues, such as water, and examine the implications for public and private sector management.

The role of the private sector could be to harvest and sell it, much as we still do now with forests. But it is public-sector scientists, like those at the National Research Council, who are measuring the impact of the last few years of drought on the water tables.

They know that it takes, as a rule of thumb, 1,000 tons of water to produce one ton of grain. Given our present farming practices, we could deplete thousands of aquifers within a generation. Is water a resource for buying and selling, or is it a public-policy concern that will require public-sector science, future management and continual regulation?

So, "grasshopper," make sure that your decision between a public or private-sector career is based on something more than an advertisement in the newspaper. I would advocate that you try them both and yet be aware of the differences. The differences you discern, and the decisions you make, should, ideally, be predicated upon your values, beliefs, interests and attitudes. In other words, what you end up doing for most of the next thirty years — in your work life or career — and where you end up doing it will, I hope, be based upon what you most care about!

Note: As this little book is a series of letters, the author requires a recipient. Rilke addressed his listener as "my dear X." This does not work for me. As a young man, my first introduction to the concept of mentor was the old television series, Kung Fu. The young acolyte was nicknamed "grasshopper." It kept rising to the surface as I wrote this book and I decided to steal it.

1 • History

AN OLD STORY SUGGESTS THAT THE PHARAOHS OF EGYPT to sustain their culture, the remnants of which can still be seen in the Nile valley, probably created the first formal public service. The kings of Egypt had many projects, and by far the largest was that society's version of "Forest Lawn"…the pyramids! Thousands of public-sector workers and their managers were involved in what would become one of the largest bureaucracies ever created. One special feature of the pyramids was their secret tunnels, designed with the intention that no one would ever find the final resting place of each pharaoh or king. I can't help but surmise that this may represent the real beginnings of bureaucratic thinking. The tunnels were to remain a secret. Ergo, the public-sector workers building them had to be killed in order to preserve the secret. No long term employment, no pension schemes, and exceedingly short retirements!

So, once the rumour was out and evidence, perhaps, of its truth, apparent, how quickly do you think the pyramids got built? Can you imagine the following exchange?

"Yo, Ari, how are things going in the northwest quadrant of the tunnel?"

"Not so bad, Akbar, but I believe we should call for another materials feasibility study and perhaps also look into forming a committee on our mortar hauling process." Bureaucracy was born! This is a poor joke and historically inaccurate as it was slaves who did the bulk of heavy lifting but the point remains that bureaucratic behaviour goes way back.

Public service history is as old as governance, and it is as good or bad as you believe it to be. As the structure of human societies has changed — from tribal factions through monarchies to elected leaders — so too has public service necessarily been forced to adapt and change. It has oppressed,

Bureaucratically Incorrect

and it has liberated. It has stifled societies, and it has helped civilizations to develop.

In our own country, public service has a most widely respected history. I imagine the first public servants in Canada as those serving and influencing early First Nation's governments such as the Six Nations. They would have served the community as well as the chief, and were specialists in health, education and defence. Their combined influence had an impact on Jefferson and Franklin as they crafted the American democracy. War has always had an effect on public service. In fact, warriors and armies have made a significant impact on the size and structure of public service for centuries. Military forces provided the first real models of organizational structure, which continues to influence our organization of public service to this day. In my own organization, we still have "officers" led by a "Director General!"

In our colonial period, the public sector was modelled after the Old Country. With Confederation in 1867, we came into our own with the *Canada Civil Service Act* of 1868. From then until the first Great War in 1914–18, our civil service struggled against the strong pressures of patronage and political influence. We went on to introduce and establish the principle of merit and diminish the role of nepotism and patronage. World events acted to further shape our public service. For example, during the Depression there were years spent trying to get rid of staff and decrease the role of public servants. During the war years (1939–45) public service was dominated by the *War Measures Act*, whose influence was to concentrate power and authority in central agencies such as Finance, Treasury Board and the Privy Council Office. Following WWII, Canada entered into a rebuilding mode, and the emphasis became one of growth and recruitment in the public service. Commissions such as the Glassco Commission in 1962 began to introduce concepts like management reform and collective bargaining.

Contemporary public service, just as it was in earlier times, has been impacted by economics (recessions), politics, union activity, the courts and public sentiment. Recent efforts on public sector improvement such as PS 2000 and La Releve indicate a much more thoughtful, professional and "Made in Canada" approach to civil service reform. The more active

Bureaucratically Incorrect

role of the Auditor General has helped to guide reform in a more positive direction.

This is just a brief, thumbnail sketch of public service as it grew. The public service of today has obviously changed much during the past 100 years. Some changes have been effective, while others perhaps not so much. Your work as a young public servant today is obviously quite different from the work, say, of an account clerk in the Immigration Department back in 1912. Or is it? You dress differently. You have different machinery on your desk, and you probably have a different relationship with your boss, but some things remain fundamentally the same.

You both serve *citizens*. You both work in an area of very important public policy. You have the same ministerial masters today as then — the Cabinet Minister in the House and the Deputy Minister and senior executives in your office.

The changes have more to do with what Peter Senge — in his work on learning organizations — calls "mental models" or ways of seeing the world. Assumptions, beliefs and theories become a fixed way of understanding the world around us. They can be so powerful that they actually inhibit new learning. To give you an understanding of the power of mental models, here is a little story about my early days as a public servant in the education sector. As a school superintendent, one of my duties was to supervise university students in their internships. I considered myself a progressive sort of guy, and looked for innovative approaches in the classroom. Keep in mind that this was a about twenty years ago — in the early 1980's — when university students were encouraged to practice child-centred learning, individualized instruction and creative approaches to curriculum and programming.

I would come into their classrooms and see the kids in straight rows, notes on the board and a lecture on the go. It was like 1956. I took my frustration to an old professor and friend at the university. "You have had these people for four years at the university," I implored, "yet they come into my schools looking and performing like teachers from my own childhood."

He listened to my point of view, calmed me down, and explained quietly that yes, he'd had them for four years, but before that, the school system had them for twelve years. For twelve long years, they had sat in those hard little desks, observing and integrating the behaviour of teachers — creating a mental model, if you will, of what a teacher is and does. The sorry part is that four years of innovative thinking at college could not entirely replace the mental model they had constructed and, under pressure, students reverted to the default.

Mental models are ubiquitous, and we should be clear from the outset that there are plenty of mental models being applied in public service. Starting with yours!

Whether or not you are aware of it, you began your employment with a fundamental preconception about the public service — this formed by your upbringing, parenting, family of origin, education, work experience, friends, the print and broadcast media to which you are exposed and the person you love. Your future impact on the public service will be influenced, in part, by your ability to set aside whatever particular mental models you now carry. Your willingness to embrace new mental models and stay open and receptive to continuous learning will be necessary for you to make a difference and contribute to our public service history.

Think about it. Your supervisor or manager has a mental model of public service. The citizens you serve have their own mental models as well. Politicians have a definite mental model about public service. Your father-in-law has one. A union steward has one. Some of these mental models may be positive whereas others, perhaps, are not so helpful or accurate.

Common mental models imposed on us include the belief that city hall does not listen to citizens, we are addicted to paper and forms and long line ups are how we do business. These are just a few of our historical mental models which may or may not be true, fair, realistic or consistently experienced by all.

One explanation for an especially long period of time when the image of the public service image suffered is "it was the Sixties." Sure, why not? We blame everything else on the Sixties, and we Sixties products are often seen as leaving the noxious legacy of our own profligate baby boomer generation onto your generation. Still, remember that we also gave you some good music, our environmental conscience and a better deal for women, so cut us a little slack, okay?

Anyway, under the leadership of a particularly hip Prime Minister named Pierre Trudeau, we did some interesting things in public service and we may have also made a few mistakes that left a mark on the Canadian public service. On the positive side, we hired a ton of young people — oops, that would be "tonne," as decimalization or metrication was another legacy of those times! We produced thousands of idealistic, energetic young people who were real system thinkers…individuals who wanted to change the system, not just solve problems.

The public service, to the amazement of many, stepped up and said why not join us and try to change the system from within as well as from the streets? It was quite something to behold. Street kids became community development officers. Bikers became employment counsellors. Programs were created to deal with the alienated, disadvantaged, oppressed and addicted. The public service was discovered, pushed and infiltrated. Believe me, the people and the programs of thirty years ago had a huge impact and influence upon the public service and on how it has evolved to this day.

However, we suffered from one major dilemma: we didn't know when or how to stop. The lovely jargon "sunset clause" hadn't yet been coined. If something started as a good idea, it just kept right on going. Sooner or later, you ran out of one or both of two things…vision and money!

Let's be honest here. Over the last forty years, public service did get bloated, became ineffective or redundant in many areas, and largely lost its sense of direction.

Mental models, paradigms or huge assumptions were starting to be formed. The notion of what a public service should look like was ripe for challenge.

In the eighties, the chickens came home to roost. The steel cage match up of a portly, slow-moving public service met up with a tough, steel-toed bully called "downsizing." This led to a brawl from which scars are still visible and skirmishes still abound. Your dad or aunt may have been one of the casualties. Talk about mental models being smashed. Some of us thought we would be around until retirement. Some saw their life's work dropped like a marshmallow into a campfire. To those who despised the public service, it vindicated their suspicion and increased the siren call for further

Bureaucratically Incorrect

bloodletting. For those whose heart was in public service, it felt like a betrayal, and for some, the bitterness lingers. It was messy, and downsizing created yet another set of mental models and attitudes. It also in some cases, led to more work from less people

Then along came the millennium and a series of events that have had a significant impact on public service. Embassy attacks left civil servants dead, wounded or kidnapped. Oklahoma City and September 11 happened. On all levels mental models were smashed. Public service was beginning to feel quite different from the private sector.

Public service today continues to be rocked by change just as it is steadied through maturity. The big issues continue to be public security, economic growth, health and education, quality of life and protection of rights and freedoms. Public servants are on the front line as we hold conversations with Canadians draft improved public policy and serve citizens.

One of the finest improvements to come along in the last decade has been the move to create a visionary and values-based public service at all levels. One major premise of learning-organization theory is the need for an organization to be vision-led as much or more than it is policy-led. This has been tough for public service. For many years, policy was our deity, and Treasury Board Guidelines were the word of God...so to speak.

You would have enjoyed some of our first forays into the New World of vision making in the public sector. It was the time of great retreats, seeing executives heading off into the manicured bush with new-age gurus who challenged them to look into their own essence and try to find the soul of their department. Sometimes these vision quests turned into a two-year search for the perfect paragraph, followed by months of debate and wordsmithing over the uses of "could" or "should." Finally, it was made pretty to hang on the wall.

But we seem to be past all that now and, hopefully, at a stage where vision is more about what we are actually doing than what the wordsmiths say we would like to do.

Better work has been done on values. In a later letter, I will comment on how we have made significant progress in moving from a rules-based to a more values-based public service.

Bureaucratically Incorrect

The history of the public service in Canada has been one of constant change and improvement. We have moved from a civil service history of patronage, command and control, bureaucracy, rules and hierarchy, to a modern history of vision, values, participatory leadership and citizen-centred service.

The most important thing you need to learn about our history is best summed up by the line, "Those who do not learn from history are doomed to repeat it." We have a great history, but there is much to be done to make us greater still. That's your big job, grasshopper — not necessarily the one in your job description!

2 • Citizens

I REMEMBER LISTENING INTENTLY TO JOCELYN BOURGON, then Clerk of the Privy Council, as she gave one of her early presentations on La Releve, a major change initiative that followed another huge round of downsizing trauma in the early nineties. Although Bourgon's honesty, insight and passion for public service captivated us, the line that nailed us was, "And always remember, we do not serve *customers*; we serve citizens."

Like many of my colleagues, my reading was heavily influenced by the likes of organizational change gurus Peter Drucker and Tom Peters, whose basic tenet was to get back to the customer. The customer was king! Find new and better ways to serve the customer with speed, quality, and relevance. Do this with consistency and a smile and you and your organization will live long and prosper.

They were right — for business!

The problem was most of my colleagues and I was not in business — not in the private sector. We were in the public sector. Drucker and Peters were not really speaking our language, but we wanted to believe, so instead of translating their message into our own language, terms, and needs, we tried to change our business to fit their language. You can imagine how, with that one sentence, Madame Bourgon gave us back our language. We serve citizens, not customers.

Okay, but what does that really mean?

First it means we have to understand that our work is truly unique, not just a soft version of the private sector. How many times have you heard the phrase, "We need some real business people in there to run the government, get things straightened out"? During the 1980's, in Saskatchewan, the mercifully short-lived Conservative government of Grant Devine had as its slogan, "Open for business." By the time they were finished, the province was millions in debt and half the politicians were up on charges! The common sense business approach of the Harris government in Ontario it appears, worked well for private sector friends of the government at the expense of a decimated public service. Ontario will pay for years.

So we public servants have to know our work — the business we are in — what we do and whom we serve.

Start with little things like: citizens pay for their goods and services, not at the time when they use them, but once a year, in a lump sum payment when they pay their taxes. Citizens correctly see us as working for them, not for "a company." Citizens also realize that there is only one supplier of government service and, as such, they cannot go to a competitor. Therefore, if the service isn't working, it will have to be fixed, because there is nowhere else to go.

Citizens' knowledge and understanding of public service is generally based on one thing only...their own experience. It may be their memories are simply of lineups at the motor vehicle department, where employees seemed more concerned that forms were completed correctly and you stay behind the yellow line than meeting the needs of the public. They may recall being in a hospital admitting room feeling stressed when an injured child had to wait for forms to be completed. They are reminded of the time they were passed from one person, to a second and then a third person while on the phone. If a citizen walks through our door with any such memories, then face it my friend, we — you — are starting from zero.

It strikes me (and I hope you, as a new public servant) that the first thing we have to achieve is to develop a much better understanding of the people we serve — the citizens. During my thirty years of public service, I cannot recall a single conversation I have had with public service peers or elders about citizens — who they are, their rights, our rights, their responsibilities, and our responsibilities.

"The customer is always right" has long been a mantra of the business community. So, is the citizen always right? In many cases, yes, but what about "the citizen' who challenges the right of the tax auditor to examine his accounts for evidence of suspected fraud?

What about "the citizen" who pounds on the desk in the community police office about the neighbors' dog and all the while is running an underage bootlegging operation out of his own back door?

When a young man walks into a big box department store with a toaster and a valid receipt, the employee usually does not care who this man is, what he does for a living, or whether his intentions for returning the toaster are honorable. The customer is king! Give him his money back!

When a young man walks into a government office to apply for a passport, he is not a king; he is a citizen. He probably has the right to obtain a passport and he has a right to be served well, but he also has a responsibility. He is responsible for his behaviour as a citizen. A passport is not a toaster. Sure we charge a fee for the issuance of a passport — $90 each, these days — but if we grant one to someone who does not really have the right to one, someone who wants to use it fraudulently, or intends to change the photo and send it to his cousin overseas, then we have a problem and a responsibility, because we are always serving two citizens: the one across the desk and his neighbour — or the public, the collective.

The difference I see between a customer and a citizen lies in our expectations. A customer expects fair exchange for their money. A citizen expects us to provide services for his tax dollars but, at the same time, expects us to protect both his interests as well as those of the community in which he lives.

This additional responsibility places a greater weight on our shoulders, for sure, but it doesn't have to be a weight that immobilizes us. I am convinced that it is precisely this dual responsibility that has — far too often — contributed to the removal of "service" from "public service" over the years.

Let's try and get one more thing straight.

We can agree to use the word "citizen" in place of the word "customer," but the word "service" shall remain — and hopefully continue to be strengthened.

Public service is the front line of governance and we are charged with two fundamental responsibilities: service and regulation. A police department provides protection as a service, but must also enforce the Criminal Code and regulations under the law.

A tax assessor may oblige you and serve you well in obtaining your refund within fourteen days, but must still uphold the Income Tax Act.

Public service can get into difficulty whenever concerns over or enforcement of regulations succeeds only in hampering or choking our ability to deliver high-quality, fast and effective service. The push and pull between service and regulation is the dichotomy upon which most of our reputation and history — our story — has been built. "What can I do for you today, sir?" You want a permit to move that building onto another site? Well, let me see now. We will have to look at the building code, check with the transportation authority, obtain a police permit and seek clearance from the power company."

"Fine, how long will all of this take?" the citizen asks.

Now, this is the point where the "service" part of "public service" either kicks in…or doesn't!

Public Servant "A" grimaces and looks down at his desk. "This could take a while. Lately, we've been having trouble with the permit boys downstairs, and the power company is behind on their approvals. Gosh, I can't say for sure, but I hope you are not in too much of a hurry."

Public Servant "B," looks him in the eye and says, "No problem. We'll get started right away. Let's get one of the guys from permits downstairs on the phone and have him come up here and sit with you on that part. As he talks to you, I will phone the transport people and the police department and get appointments set up for you for later this afternoon. Let's see how fast we can get this off the ground."

Okay, you're thinking, I want to be Public Servant "B," but it strikes me that no matter how much I want to give this citizen the best service, I am still at the mercy of the system, the boys in the basement, and all the other departments and jurisdictions.

You are right! You are at their mercy, especially if you have not done your homework. Have you built a process map for the moving of a house? Did you build it with all your partners and systems-representatives in the same room? Once you built that map, did you work on it as a group until you eliminated the time constraints, excess approvals, non-value-added paperwork and bottlenecks?

You see, grasshopper, no one is asking us to skip the accountability process or, as some of our elders used to do, find a back door. No, we must still do the right thing. What we want to try and avoid is to serve process for process' sake or people's egos.

Before we can provide that "good service" to citizens, we have to know that we have fine-tuned the system to allow us to provide the most effective service to each citizen.

There is nothing more miserable than the public service employee who wants to do well, wants to help, wants to be friendly, wants to get it done more quickly, but is as much a victim of poor process and practice as the citizen doing a slow burn on the other end of the line!

My advice would be, do not become another rebel server. You know what I mean. A rebel server is one who takes the citizen aside, lowers her voice and whispers words of support and condolence. Yes, this outfit doesn't know its head from a hole in the ground. And hey, I know this guy. Don't tell anybody I sent you…"

This does not serve the citizen.

Your first responsibility is to clean up and get your house in order. You have got to clean the floor, organize the tools, and get everyone on schedule. Fix the priorities and build a good system first. Oh, and another thing. Once you get that system fixed and running smooth like a well-oiled clock, tear it apart and rebuild it again. Times change and everything that was once improved upon can always be improved upon again.

We began this chapter by explaining how public service can get into difficulty by trying too much to be like business. Let us be a bit careful here.

The problem usually stems from trying to run public service like a business, with business principles and values. This does not work well.

Business practices are another kettle of fish altogether. There are so many good business practices available to choose from (like the aforementioned process mapping) — practices generic in their application. They don't care whom you serve or what your business involves. They exist only to help you do what you do, and do it better.

We serve citizens, not customers, but the bottom line is that we *serve*.

3 • Governance

*I*AM NOT PARTICULARLY PROUD OF WHAT I AM ABOUT TO CONFESS HERE, but in thirty years of public service, I have never really understood how the government, which employs me, actually works! There are a number of reasons for this — and none are particularly good excuses for my lack of understanding.

For one thing, the only formal way to learn how government works has been to take a class on the topic. Such classes have typically been offered only to public service employees selected for management training. Having never been on such a track — or even a footpath — I have yet to experience such a course. So that was perhaps...mistake number one!

It just never seemed all that important. People would toss around phrases like cabinet document or ministerial accountability or social contract and I would nod sagely, smart enough to have a general idea of what these meant, just not wise enough to have a clue as to their real meaning. Personal mistake, number two!

A great deal of this information was available somewhere, wasn't it? If only one could be motivated to and find it. It had to be available somewhere because my bosses had to get it from somewhere, right? And hey, there are libraries, and for almost the last twenty years, the Internet and World Wide Web has been loading up with a lot of good material in this domain as well. Personal mistake number three!

It wasn't in my job description, so I was not offered the course. It didn't seem important, so I faked my way through the conversations and finally, let's face it, I didn't have the ambition to go out and get the knowledge myself as an active, continuous learner might have done.

So there you have it. Do as I now suggest, not as I did.

Bureaucratically Incorrect

I can tell you now that understanding how government — your employer — works, and subsequently how public service serves that governance model is, as the Ford Motor Company used to say, "Job One."

I would have been a much better teacher, serving parents and students so much more effectively, if I had taken the time to learn and understand how a school board works. The governance model of a school board affects everything you do — the curriculum being taught, your rights and responsibilities as an employee, the rights of students and parents and the impact of government decisions. I would have known why — at times — we had no authority to develop local curriculum, or why a program was really being cut. Perhaps these events actually reflected Ministry funding formulas rather than our faulty perception of a tight-fisted local board.

As a provincial employee working within the Ministry of Environment, I would have had a much clearer understanding of federal-provincial water agreements on water rights, funding transfers and the regulatory guidelines around fish and water fowl management.

As an employee of a First Nations government, I would have recognized a wider range of opportunities for governance needing to be crafted as opposed to handed down. I regret not learning more about the key Acts and legislation that govern First Nations. A greater and wider knowledge could have made me more helpful in ameliorating the impacts and frustration citizens experience when they are involved in effecting change through various — federal, provincial, municipal and First Nations — levels of government. I would have been much more effective in helping to explore and create new approaches to crafting models of local governance that reflected local history, culture and beliefs.

My employment experience and history with the federal government has also been full of ignorance about governance.

One of the great difficulties we all face in working for the federal system of governance is the distance we may find ourselves from the centre of action — Ottawa. If you are a municipal or First Nations employee, headquarters is often just down the street. A provincial employee may be a few hours' drive away from headquarters — the provincial legislature or provincial government department building. If you don't live in Ottawa, a federal employee generally has to board a plane and take a long, food-free flight to that centre of the universe!

If the opportunity to travel and the requirement to be in close touch with headquarters is not formally part of your job, it is easy to adopt the out-of-sight, out-of-mind principle in your thinking about Ottawa. We often develop, over a period of time a bit of an attitude about our nation's capital. You know what I am talking about. The further away the seat of governance, the bigger the target. Don't get sucked into this mindset.

All my life in public service, I was a rebel without a clue. I could tell you in a heartbeat what was wrong with the system but, in all honesty, I didn't know the system. Let me say that again: You can only begin to know what is wrong with the system when you start to really know the system.

For example, every time I wanted to do something different or innovative, it seemed like the number one reason always given as to why I couldn't...was...Treasury Board Guidelines! For decades, I saw the Treasury Board as some heavy, bloated, miserable, out-of-touch gulag that existed only to make miserable my front-line, real-world life of service.

Finally, years later, I know that the Treasury Board is not a big, hoary beast — well; not entirely, anyway!

When I began to visit Ottawa and paid a little more attention, I can remember when I eventually visited the Treasury Board offices and found a whole department committed to examining how the principles of quality management could be incorporated in the public service. No one in my department had ever heard about this initiative. As I think about this, I find myself wondering what has happened in the interim and what happened to that particular project?

So, what is my point?

Well, if I could start over in my career, I would like to have had a greater knowledge of the system of governance — of which I was becoming a part.

I would want to know what ministerial accountability was and how it manifests itself. I would want to know more precisely the role of central agencies. Heck, for years, I would have loved to know what a central agency really was! I would want to know how a bill gets passed in the federal system, how a regulation gets approved in a provincial legislature, how a bylaw gets

Bureaucratically Incorrect

through a city council and how a band council resolution affects the governance on a reserve.

I would have been fascinated with the roles and responsibilities of the Clerk of the Privy Council, a Deputy Minister, the Clerk of the Legislatures, a town clerk and a band administrator. Interesting, isn't it, how many of the most powerful jobs in public service involve "clerks?"

I would have benefited by knowing how revenue was collected at the federal, provincial, municipal and band levels and how the revenue was designated for spending priorities.

How does money move from one level of government to another? Do they have gold debit cards? What is accrual accounting? Exactly what services — such as broadcasting and mail — are under federal authority or jurisdiction? What services — such as natural resources, health care and education — are under provincial authority, or jurisdiction? For what services — such as agriculture and immigration — does federal government share power, authority and responsibility with provincial governments? What is the social union agreement? How does a law get made? How does a policy get made? What is strategic planning, really? What is the expenditure management system? How does lobbying work? What about this tenuous relationship between the politician and public servant? What is Hansard? What is the rule of law? Where does the Treasury Board get its money? Who do I really work for?

It goes on and on. I don't mean to overwhelm or under whelm you on this stuff, grasshopper.

All I mean to say is that I hope you pay more attention — and do so earlier in your career — than I did. Take it piece by piece and, if I may say so, don't wait for a course. A course will be at best a minimum of three excitement-filled days. They will give you a binder with a heft of at least three inches and ten pounds. A lot of stuff…good stuff, but a bit too much. Wait till you get into management for the ubiquitous course. They pay you more then because you will suffer more. For now, take small bites, like "how to make a policy." Form a learning team, do your own research on the Internet or in the library, and have some great conversations as you learn more about the fascinating process you have chosen to be a part of.

4 • Learning

ONTEMPORARY ATTITUDES TO BOTH personal as well as organizational learning have not been quite as progressive as was first anticipated.

To fully understand the role of learning, grasshopper, we have to return to the old days for a minute. When I was a young man, learning was regarded as a "phase" you went through. The institutionalization of education led to the understanding that one literally got through the learning phase and then was rewarded with a pass into real life.

For many, the institutional culture of learning often led to distaste for learning. Getting through high school and perhaps college were, for many, an endurance run that led to graduation, after which the student comforted him or herself with the assurance that it was all over and, thank goodness, they'd never have to go back down that road.

This notion of learning as dissociated from the rest of life was first and best challenged by early radical thinkers in the field of adult education. Both women and men — such as Father Moses Coady in Nova Scotia — realized that without literacy and continuous learning, adult workers would never have a chance to rise above their present lot or hang onto their jobs in tough times.

Adult learning assumed many forms, including the early farm broadcasts on CBC radio. Frontier College was established in 1899 to bring literacy to the Canadian Pacific Railway's section gangs and lumber camps. Later, they brought university extension courses into rural and remote parts of Canada. This was called adult education because of the audience it served, but it was soon known more commonly as continuing education because the world of adults was not the world of schools and desks, this new learning had to go beyond the conventional notions. Today, we use the phrase lifelong learning to describe the new mental model around learning.

It's hard to imagine that anyone is not up to speed on this. Unfortunately, there are still a few people around who believe they have done their time learning and there is, for them, nothing else to learn.

Also be aware that lifelong learning does not have to mean a lifetime spent in classrooms and training rooms. God forbid anyone such a fate. More and more, we are looking for ways to integrate lifelong learning into the family, community and workplace.

In 2002, the federal public service finally implemented a public service policy on lifelong learning for all employees. As we know, once something becomes policy, it can be either the breath of life or the kiss of death for the idea or initiative. Policies are important but even more important is the culture that develops out of those polices. Lifelong learning must be more than just a policy; it must be a way of working and living.

My generation saw learning and training primarily as just another item on the agenda to be managed. When people went away on training it was usually seen as a problem and their training costs were not seen as recoverable. I can remember a time when learning was actually used as a punishment. We could always tell if someone had really screwed up because they were sent on educational leave, assigned French training or given the dreaded "special assignment." All three punishments, of course, had extremely high learning curves.

We also tended to see organizational learning through a universal lens — that of training. All learning activity was reduced to this one-dimensional model of training. I need to be careful in how I proceed here. There is a fine and honorable place for training. I gained some insight into the difference between training and learning from a retired Canadian Forces officer. Here's how he explained the difference between the two: "I need to be trained, Bob, on how to take my rifle apart, clean it, oil it and put it back together again, so that it fires safely and accurately. Train me to do that, with a course, an instructor and perhaps a manual of instruction. But, the on-the-ground know-how of when to pick up that rifle, whether or not to point it at somebody, and whether or not pull the trigger — that knowledge is learned, not in a classroom, not from one instructor and not from a manual."

Training is a moment; learning is a lifetime.

Bureaucratically Incorrect

So this too is part of the dilemma for organizations, especially public-sector organizations: Because our mental model of learning was formed in schools, we tend to bring that into our organizations. And because "training" best fits that model, to this day we look to training even if we agree that the concept of lifelong learning is better.

You will have to resist this tendency, unless of course, your needs fit the old colonel's definition.

If you agree that we live and work in an Age of Information and our economy is now driven by knowledge and that public service, fundamentally, lies within the knowledge sector — ergo we are all knowledge workers — here is the kicker. The Industrial Age required little knowledge from the majority of its workers. Knowledge was left to the managers, the planners and the efficiency experts. Knowledge and information was broken up, like the system, into smaller, more manageable pieces.

In the public service environment, we realize we cannot break policy development into small pieces and divide front-line service into bite-sized chunks. We cannot protect only parts of the public, we protect the whole. Public service, more than ever, has to be seen, understood and delivered as a system. As public servants, we need to be great practitioners of systems thinking. We have to believe that the intelligence, innovation and effectiveness of public service are as critical to and available at the front lines as ever it was or is in the boardrooms.

We also have to believe that the source of knowledge lies within all of us, not just in the teachers in the training room. Most importantly, we need to understand that by sharing knowledge throughout the organization and beyond that a true learning culture will arise. I have already made a grave error by suggesting that learning could somehow be restricted to one chapter in this book. Learning is the book. It is the whole.

If the number one tool of the Industrial Age was the assembly line, then the number one tool of the Knowledge Age is lifelong learning.

We are going to have to free our minds for this one, if we truly want the public service to be leaders in the knowledge revolution, rather than always trying to catch up to it.

Young public servants must demand — and help build — learning cultures, not simply learning programs in their organizations. Public service loves programs, but programs in a fast-paced knowledge/information age become obsolete faster than beanie babies.

Learning organizations are, as they say, nimble, responsive and forward thinking. Citizens have the right to nimble, responsive and far-sighted public service.

So is it all about fresh, new and cutting-edge stuff? Of course not! Remember some of our previous conversations around values?

There is your constant. Values. Citizens also expect consistency in their public service. This can be accomplished only by acknowledging and serving public-service values.

The role of lifelong learning is to find better ways of delivering service within the constant of relevant and timeless values.

Where it gets a little sticky, I suppose, is where we find that the values of the society also change. But hey, without a culture of lifelong learning, we could find ourselves out of sync on values as well as with practice.

Elsewhere in this book, you will find I mention a variety tools, ideas and approaches to lifelong learning. Right now, however, you need to get your head around one major thought. Lifelong learning takes place in a workplace culture, not in a workplace policy or program. If you get this, then you know what you have to do.

You must contribute to that culture. You will do this, first of all, by becoming a lifelong learner yourself. You will stop seeing your workday in segments of work and segments of study. You will spend your day in a bubble of working and learning. Everything you do will be tested against your learning. Everything you learn will be tested against the work to be done.

You will be as strategic about your learning as you are about your work.

You will be a sponge.

You will soak up knowledge from your elders, colleagues and clients. You will benchmark your work against the best in practice continuously.

You will track down the information and knowledge required, becoming the best at what you do.

You will contribute to a culture of learning on your team.

You will never be fully satisfied because, as a learner, on a learning team, in a learning organization, you know in your heart that your team could have done it better if they'd known....

Next time, we will know more and we can know more because we can always learn.

Bureaucratically Incorrect

5 • A Story

I AM ALWAYS FASCINATED WHEN I GET A PEEK into what I call the secret life of public servants. The exterior so often does not really reflect the interior.

One day I was working with a small group of public servants that were involved with the information technology side of things. As you're about to learn, I have my own particular mental models about people who dig into their work in small bytes instead of big bites.

I think we were working on building a team charter. At the break, I got into a conversation with one of the other participants about some aspect of the computer world. He may have noticed my eyes starting to roll. "Actually, that's not what I wanted to talk to you about anyway," says this fellow. "I am really interested in your ideas on the balance between teaching and learning in a learning organization." Then he told me a little about himself.

Apparently, he had been a classical musician in a former life. He had studied and taught in Berkeley, California. My eyes opened a little wider. I'm thinking, what the heck are you doing here playing with keyboards, when you could be playing with…well, keyboards? Anyway, I cannot remember his name or what he played, but he went on to tell me a wonderful story about how the great violinist Jascha Heifitz — who was also teaching at Berkeley. The music faculty would get together frequently on a social basis and, since this was California, hot tubs were part of the culture. As a faculty member, this fellow often found himself soaking in the company of great musicians — all fuelled by spirits and fine food. One night, while they were all in the tub, including the revered Heifitz, the conversation turned to teaching. One faculty member asked the great man, "Sir, you are one of the most renowned artists in the world. You can do whatever you want. Why do you still teach?"

Heifitz turned and responded softly but with great clarity, "I teach because when I teach, I get better."

I love that! Remember grasshopper, the more you teach, the more you will learn. Start soon.

6 • Teamwork

THE WORD "TEAM" HAS CREATED MORE HAVOC in the Metaphor Hall of Fame than just about any other word, with the possible exception of "paradigm." A colleague related the following story.

We had a manager who returned one Friday afternoon from an executive seminar and, with a highly motivated gleam in his eye, called us together for the following announcement. Though we had been the "Northwest Unit" for the past twenty-three years, as of Monday we would be known as the "Northwest Team!"

So what happened between Friday and Monday? You are right, nothing! We didn't even get T-shirts or jackets. All we got was a new name; everything remained exactly as it had always been.

Today, we can still have a situation where a newly enlightened manager will probably return to the office ready and anxious to share the virtues of one of the personality type tests they just went through in a team building seminar. Employees will probably enjoy doing the tests as well. They will gain some better insight into how we are all different in our styles but by itself, the final impact on daily workload may not really amount to very much.

So what's the deal with this team stuff, anyway? Personally, grasshopper, I think it could be the real deal! Trouble is, we oversimplify it by expecting things to change as a result of thinking good thoughts, or being more kind to each other, or having gained some insight into personality differences among our co-workers. Alternately, we complicate it by adopting an academic approach, in which we analyze each other to the nth degree.

Do you know any mailroom teams that, in the midst of struggling and biting at each other during a serious time and deadline crunch, stop and engage in a little team feedback about whether they are now moving from the storming to the norming phase of their team development? Not very likely!

More research has probably been undertaken on team analysis tools than on any other aspect of work life. You can measure team cohesiveness, chart individual contributions and roles and "measure" members' personality traits. These are all good things.

However, in my experience, their impact on front-line teamwork has been minimal. So what works? Three basic approaches have always helped to improve any team of which I have been a member.

First, you have to build respect for individuals before you can build respect for the team. A pitiful irony is the dysfunctional group made up of individuals who can't stand each other, but pin their hopes on teamwork exercises. Another nasty little spin-off is an emerging attitude that only the group is important, and everyone must conform to the group — be a team player and so on.

A team that does not or cannot respect the individual and promote strong independent thinking can never be a high-performing team. A strong team does not stifle the individual; it provides support, nurtures and rewards each member's efforts. The success of personal effort with group support, leads to accomplishments that reflects well on both the individual and the team.

The second tough approach to becoming a real team is in understanding the shift from jobs to work. Remember our conversation about the shift from the Industrial Age, where work was broken down into specific jobs, and the Knowledge Age, marked as it is by an emerging need to see the whole picture of work needing to be done? Well, the latter is critical to team development. Think about it. Is the work in your area seen as belonging to everyone, including the drudge stuff, or do you still see it as Jean's stuff, Bill's projects and so on? Now hang on a moment. I see you are getting a bit excited. I am not saying Jean cannot have her own area of expertise and responsibility. What I am implying is that while she holds leadership in that area, in a true team approach, we all have responsibilities that support, build and add value to that work. Our responsibilities are all strengthened by her leadership. In thirty years, I've contributed more than my share of personal work-plans, but have rarely engaged in teamwork planning. The unit plan was generally an accumulation of our individual plans. Lately, I've been more impressed with a teamwork plan that builds effectiveness and group power by fostering the leadership initiative of each member of the team. Teams need repeated opportunities to hold conversations about "how" they will get the work done and how they will work together. This, in my experience, has been the missing link in developing effective teams. Things like work planning — compliance stuff — we do well, and we can usually pull it off under tight deadlines. But, how we intend to get things done, to what standards, and with what tools and with whose commitment...whew, that's not really talked about much around here. Big assumptions get made.

And there's the rub. To become a real team, you have to talk to one another. No, not just more staff meetings. And please, no more internal communication studies. We may even start to wean ourselves off those constant team-building workshops.

I hate to say it again, but this one really is so simple: Try talking to each other — every day!

A daily standup meeting (fifteen minutes in the morning before starting work) could help. Talk to one another when a problem occurs. Team workouts (focused problem solving sessions) could help you with this. Talk to each other about your values, goals, service standards, protocols and improvement strategies. The information such conversations reveal could result in a draft of a team charter.

Remember, conversation is the lifeblood of knowledge. The more frequent the conversational exchange, the greater the knowledge shared or pooled. A monthly staff meeting is not enough; it's like living with a tourniquet cutting off vital intelligence flow to the brain.

Some words of caution as well, grasshopper. Teamwork does not necessarily imply friendship, closeness or affection. My goodness, I dreaded the bosses who would take us to lunch or their house or a bar for an annual drink. You knew they really hated to converse with us, but once a year — they could bite the bullet and do it for the cause. Even worse were the bosses who realized the team was going off the rails, and believed that by bringing us home for dinner, they would somehow salvage the morale of the group.

Hey, we know each other just fine. That's sometimes even the problem. What we don't know is how to work with each other. Frankly, I believe Eddy to be an egomaniac, Rose to be a prude, Rhonda to be a workaholic and Jeremy to be bone-lazy. I know them just fine; it's working with them that gives me trouble. A nice pasta lunch at a Greek restaurant every Christmas isn't going to make me like or dislike these people any more or less. Help me find a way to get past the personal stuff we can't change, and into the work stuff that we can change. Teamwork, it seems to me, is a systems issue once again. Many team gurus have tried to make it an issue around personality and attitudes. I believe that cougar has been treed enough already. The critical word in teamwork is not "team," but "work." How we work together has to "trump" how we get along together.

When I talk to people, their chief complaints are usually around workload, effectiveness and relevance. People generally love to work. Sometimes they even love their job. Where they get into difficulty is in tripping over one another, dealing with red tape, misunderstanding roles and responsibilities, and feeling that not everyone is on the same page — which might be a result of lack of alignment and little or no clarity on accountability.

A high-performing team tackles the work, not the personal relationships on the team. Continual conversations about activities, goals, improvements and, of course, rewards, not only make a team more effective, but — get this — remember those personalities, attitudes and behaviours we thought were the problem? Well, now that we are talking every day, solving problems together, planning as a team, smashing bottlenecks and process snags, hey, we are actually starting to like each other a bit more.

But be prudent; let it go. Stick to the work, the teamwork.

7 • Technology

SO, GRASSHOPPER, I ENJOYED YOUR LAST NOTE even if it was on the e-mail. Who am I kidding? No one uses any other kind of mail these days. So upon receiving your last e-mail, I have been thinking that I should reflect a little more on my aversion (well known by my colleagues) to the e-mail beast. In fact this whole field of technology is probably where I should be looking to you for some guidance. Actually, I have. It is wonderful to peek over your shoulder and see your skill, comfort and ease with technology. And I believe the futurists when they predict a new generation is coming who will undertake most, if not all of its business electronically.

I can in truth, relate to the emerging world of e-government. I can see how it has already made a huge impact on our systems and processes. I love my taxes going out online and my refund returning at warp speed. It already is and will continue to be advanced technology such as this that will radically change how public servants wage peace in foreign countries, protect citizens from bad guys, and diagnose illness in citizens in remote communities. So I do get it, okay?

I listened to a radio report that suggested how we could use computer simulations to build models to enhance our study of viruses. Soon, we'll find ways to combat such monsters as the Ebola virus without actually having to deal with the actual pathogen under potentially hazardous, albeit strict laboratory conditions. I know a lot of public-service scientists who will feel a lot safer with this type of technological breakthrough.

Undoubtedly, technology will be a first-string player in any learning organization. Technology will connect us to emerging knowledge all over the world.

So why am I still struggling with the ever-present desktop, the incessant cell phones, the delicious Blackberry and the showoff PowerPoint?

Let me inject what may seem to be a point that is a wee bit off track. Most of us were brought up with the old maxim that most things are fine in moderation; only when we overuse or abuse do we get into difficulty. A glass of wine with meals is considered healthy; one or two bottles a day may lead to a spot of trouble. A few chips and dip on Friday night with a movie, okay. An oversize bag of deep-fried potato chips and a 32-ounce pop on the subway every day after work indicates something may be amiss.

My grandmother just celebrated her 101st birthday. She remembers planes when they had two wings, on top of one another. I am fifty-seven. I remember school copiers that ran on alcohol — not unlike a few of the teachers in those days.

Anyway, the Gestetner Duplicating Machine was quite revolutionary when it was introduced in the late nineteenth century. Offices, schools and businesses could see a new future, freed from the tyranny of dreaded carbon paper. Carbon paper? Look it up in a history book or somewhere on the Internet, grasshopper. I'm short of time here.

So, this was the big technology breakthrough for me in my first public service job as a teacher in the Far North. I was introduced to the Gestetner, trained on the Gestetner, then I used the Gestetner.

Actually, I didn't use it very much.

But let me tell you, there were Gestetner freaks in those schools. I recall the lineups! You almost had to book time on the thing. What was a pretty good tool for, say, duplicating a math quiz, was now being used in every subject.

Ask someone who was a school kid in those days. With one teacher, it could be a day of kids painting their own paintings, writing their own stories, doing their own research and solving some problems on their own. With other teachers, it was a day spent in a flurry of mimeograph sheets. Fast, easy and one-size-fits-all for the teacher, of course. Boring, repetitious and lacking in an ounce of creativity for the student.

These teachers were classic mimeograph abusers.

A little in moderation would have worked fine. "A lot" became a crutch and a habit. Now let's fast-forward to the present and a new, more contemporary "mimeograph." We call it PowerPoint.

Ian Parker, writing in the *New Yorker*, observed, "Before there were presentations, there were conversations, which were a little like presentations but with fewer bullet points, and no one had to dim the lights." David Weinburger commented in *The Cluetrain Manifesto*, "You can only have a conversation if you are not afraid to be wrong. Otherwise, you are not conversing; you're just disclaiming, speechifying or reading what is on the PowerPoint. To converse, you have to be willing to be wrong in front of another person."

In today's corporate boardroom, the executive without PowerPoint is made to feel like a short order cook without a hairnet. Not only do we feel we need it to deliver our message, but more insidiously, we are starting to feel adjudicated by the PowerPoint presentation itself as much as or even more than the content of the presentation itself. You can hear the boardroom muttering bristling with, "Why doesn't this guy use the zoom feature like the last woman?" Or, "I hope he has a video clip to break up all this text."

PowerPoint is the latest incarnation in a long evolution including the aforementioned superannuated mimeograph machine, morphing into the overhead projector, the slide show and finally the computerized slide and video show.

What makes this particular technological advance so addictive?

Well, for a start, how about fear? Anxiety is a pretty big motivator. There is a long and common list of really horrifying things that people fear, and public speaking comes pretty close to the top. Trouble is, public speaking is a critical or core competency on many corporate job descriptions. This is especially true for those higher up in the food chain. So, along comes the Age of the Presentation with the expedient technology that says, "Hey, give me the essence of what you want to say; I will distill it into easy points and you can present it in the dark without fear of people looking right at you. Now, with your well-covered corporate persona, you can push the buttons and read the message with no fear of mistakes."

Bureaucratically Incorrect

The New York Times reported that the board investigating the space shuttle disaster not only fingered the insulation problem but held responsible PowerPoint as well. It seems that the scientists were moving away from the culture of reading scientific papers for their knowledge and were relying more and more on the PowerPoint presentation for their information. I guess the top ten bullet points are not enough to keep things in the air.

At about the same time we became struck with the technological presentation model, we also started to see the emergence of experts in communications, public relations and marketing. These people were hired to simplify what the organization (not the people in the organization) had to say. We entered the era of "key messages, press releases, and wordsmithing." More and more, it became an anathema to feel that one might make a mistake in public. Subsequently, no one wanted to speak up, out of fear that their own words would come back to bite them on their tender assets!

Once again, slides and PowerPoint came to the rescue. Vetted to the finest degree, worked on for days and weeks by more writers than a Harbourfront author's workshop, the presentation is finally deemed ready to go. The presenter's confidence is now firmly embedded within the presentation, much more so than in his or her head.

Still, there is some lingering discomfort. The call goes out to the PowerPoint elves. I need more excitement. Can you jazz it up a little? There is not enough motivation in this thing. Or even the fallacious enjoinder, "Can you get a bit more passion into this?" As well, we have the disquieting image of a six-figure executive poring over a presentation, suggesting font changes, spotting grammatical mistakes and changing screen colours.

The art of conversation is one of the oldest and most durable of the arts. Conversation is at the very core of a true free market, just check out Granville Island in Vancouver or the Byword Market in Ottawa. Good conversation is also the essential substance in the creation of public policy, front-line service to customers and citizens and the exchange of knowledge and growth of nations. Good science, new products, economic growth and health reform do not come about through the exchange of presentations. The Middle East will not achieve peace through presentations. The reform of human resources management and other public and private sector changes will not come about through presentations. The school system will not be improved as a result of presentations.

Perhaps it's time to realize that big issues such as peace, economic growth, change and reform will happen only through the power of conversation. People respond best to honesty and passion. There is only one way to deliver such honesty and passion, and that is by using your own voice, with perhaps some contributing harmonic support from your body language.

Everyone has a voice of some sort, but not everyone gets to use it. In *The Cluetrain Manifesto*, the authors speculate that the Internet is giving back to millions of people their own voice. They can now rise above, go around or over the top of the existing power structures that hitherto fore limited the exercise, or reach of their voice.

The apparent irony is that technology, such as the Web, gives voice and connection, while on the ground, technology such as PowerPoint is replacing voice and connectivity with correct "messaging."

Forget about the boardroom for a minute and think about how PowerPoint is moving into the classroom. Students are beginning to feel their thinking is being judged more on the presentation than the content. And what about church services these days? Ministers and music directors are starting to dim the lights in order to project their words onto a screen. I always understood that Jesus, Mohammed and others of their business were storytellers. Each had a pretty important message to share, but somehow I doubt that they would, even today, exchange their direct stories with people for a tricked-up PowerPoint presentation.

So, I suppose that I may be paying more than necessary attention to the dark side of technology these days. Still, I am starting to think it is more than just a nuisance when a cell phone rings in the middle of an important talk. At that moment, technology has trumped conversation, and I don't believe it deserves the trump card.

I am disturbed by the stories I hear of e-mail abuse. Stories about colleagues locked into days of e-mail exchange going nowhere, over issues that could have been resolved with a half-hour of conversation over a cup of coffee.

I have been thinking lately about the young man who came to me one day, upset with how overworked he was. I thought I'd heard it all before, but this guy had a new twist. Seems he had been covering for his boss for months, doing the boss's work plus his own. He was exhausted. Why? His boss was addicted to day trading. His boss was in greed-heaven with his desktop hot-wired into a brokerage house. He started off slow, checking his stocks in the morning, then soon he got into the actual trading where the turnaround was fast and you had to stay connected all day.

Trouble!

And on it goes. We are well past the stage of a teacher using technology because he is too lazy to think of more creative ways for kids to learn. Technology on our desks and hips now allows us to indulge in speed and substance, in doses and choices that may not always be reflected in moderation.

I remember one of my first public-sector managers back in the late sixties. He was a fine gentleman by all accounts, as I recall, but he had a little habit. He "mainlined" inter-office memos.

First thing, every morning, he would go to the supply cabinet, grab a cellophane-wrapped pack of inter-office memos, and then spirit them back to his clutter-free oak desk.

I am sorry, grasshopper; of course you have no idea what an inter-office memo is. Well, imagine five colour-coded duplicate sheets of paper held statically together with carbon paper (that from your previous research).

So, there he was for most of the day behind closed doors, firing off memos...busy, busy, and busy. There were memos to self, memos to staff, memos to regional offices, memos to file, and so on. Into the out-basket they went, and out the door with his secretary (another quaint term you may want to look up on the Internet).

We called him the memo-manager.

I thought he went the way of the buffalo, until the advent of e-mail. I found him again thirty years later. Well, not him exactly, a clone of him came to life in one of my new managers. Again, the clean desk, the closed door and busyness, only this time he was hip, "with it" if you will. This guy now had e-mail to self, e-mail to staff, e-mail to regions and e-mail to file. Copies were a flick of the "cc" button and no messy carbon paper.

When I moved into a new office in Toronto in the mid eighties, I discovered to my delight that the mail was delivered by a robot. Very cool I thought. Then it just got to be a beeping, lumbering nuisance. When I heard about the interesting mentally challenged person the robot replaced, all coolness evaporated. Give me back the person!

So here is what I have learned about technology. You have to break this horse well, because it can go a hundred kilometres an hour and still get nothing done. Technology is going to be a big player in our public service work, but we must realize it offers no advantage if we find ourselves doing bad things faster or more elegantly or in greater solitude.

8 • Leadership

LEADERSHIP IS A LOT LIKE *Gingko Biloba* FOR US OLD CREAKS. We are pretty sure it may be good for us, but we haven't got a clue about what it is, where it comes from or what it is supposed to do for us.

Ever since humans sat around in caves deciding who would go outside to investigate a strange noise, leadership has been a fairly important issue. Some things have not changed since then.

For example, the woman eventually selected to check out "that noise" outside the cave was just that...selected. She may have volunteered because of some perceived innate bravery, she may have been chosen for her previous experience in dealing with strange noises. The bottom line is, nearly everyone agreed she was the one for the job.

If the people you are to lead have not accepted or given you the mantle of leadership, all you've got going is a great title on a snappy business card, and of course, a corner office with a potted palm tree.

The second simple truism, since cave days, is that the chosen leader has to accept the cloak of leadership. Leadership has not always been about office square footage and bonus pay. Sometimes, it was a matter of stepping out of the cave, aware of the risk that you might have been the first to be eaten. To accept that you may be dinner rather than being adored for coming back with dinner, has been henceforth a primary defining characteristic of leadership.

Not to oversimplify the topic, there are two areas where leadership breaks down in our modern organizations, including public service. Generally, leaders are not chosen by those who have to follow. And less surprisingly, many leaders covet the perks of leadership — more money, prestige and power — but never really accept the real weight of the leadership mantle.

They have no desire to stick their head outside the entrance of the cave; they just want their name above it.

In a previous chapter, we talked about the origins of bureaucracy, hierarchy and structural elements within organizations. The need to keep large groups of people in line led to a structure resembling a pyramid — the most powerful at the top and the least powerful at the bottom. Not all the layers could be controlled from the top, so we developed a command-and-control system at each level. In the military model of organization, we called the people charged with this function "officers." Later, the nonmilitary environments or situations, we called them "managers." Amazingly, you can still find titles like "staffing officer" in the Canadian federal public service. As I mentioned earlier, I still work for a Director General. Thankfully, saluting is optional.

Now there is a mental model that could use a little strategic rearrangement.

So the large organization creates a new class of worker, the management class. Years pass, and our innate drive for improvement led to management improvement and training. One more leap ahead to the Industrial Age, and we meet Frederick Taylor, the father of efficiency measurement and the progenitor of Scientific Management.

Taylor's premise was perfect for the Industrial Age. Take the complex whole of the work to be done, and break it into manageable pieces. We then train workers and managers to be experts in different stages of the process. We then put the whole thing back together again. The number one tool of Scientific Management became the highly efficient but personally stultifying assembly line. The fundamental management premise behind Scientific Management was the refining and polishing of the command-and-control hierarchical approach.

The people at the top decided what needed to be done, their planners determined how it would be done, and this management world-view would be pushed through the management cadre for interpretation and delegation to the individual parts of the whole.

It works fine, by the way, if the people at the top know what they are doing, and if the directives, once leaving the top, are received intact at the bottom.

I think you might already see where this is going. There are some pretty smart people at the top of many organizations, right? So let's test it out. Let's say you are a writer. You want to write a book about Canadian forest policy. You are a good writer and want to be as accurate and comprehensive as possible. So do you set up an interview with the Assistant Deputy Minister of Forests? Ask all the questions you can think of, then sit down and write the book now that you have been to the top of the mountain? Or do you conduct more than two hundred interviews with every level of manager and worker in the forestry department? And once you have finished with that, interview forest partners, including business interests, environmentalists and citizens? After all this, maybe you sit down and start to write.

I am still fascinated by the way the first approach continues to be exercised inside many public sector organizations. People sit in their cubicles waiting for the Deputy Minister to come out with a directive on this and that particular issue. They expect their manager to set the direction for the next fiscal year. We sit in meetings and try to read the thoughts of the most powerful person in the room and then re-jig our thinking accordingly.

All this may come as a shock to you, grasshopper, then again, maybe not. The base intelligence of an organization is not pooled at the top. The essence of the intelligence in an organization comes from the citizens it serves, the partners with whom it engages, the front line personnel doing the work and the front-line managers gathering and communicating the intelligence. Finally, it is in the boardrooms where the intelligence comes together to forge a view that uses all of it to make good decisions, communicate the vision and be accountable for the results.

If those in the boardroom were to rely solely on their own intelligence, the limo would be out of gas halfway through the meeting!

A second difficulty with command-and-control, top-down process is how to get those commands from on high to filter down to the bottom. This can be a lot like pushing string. There are lots of places where it can buckle and bunch up. Remember that old parlour game (of course you don't) where you generate a sentence in one part of the circle, whisper it one by one around the circle, and by the time it comes back to the originator,

Bureaucratically Incorrect

it bares little or no resemblance to the original statement? This is what usually happens with a top-down leadership model. For example, from WWII: Send reinforcements, we're going to advance becomes send three and four pence, we're going to a dance?

Furthermore, you have the problem of "buy-in." This is a phrase that drives me crazy. For me, as a front-line person, it has always meant a variation on the following: managers heading off for a few days to some fine retreat, perhaps on Vancouver Island, with a consultant and a flip chart. We were happy to see them go, as it got them out of our hair for a while, and we always seemed to accomplish more in their absence.

Back they would come, refreshed and excited, armed with a new strategic direction. They would gather us together, give us a PowerPoint presentation of their work and, with straight faces, announce that all they needed now for everything to work perfectly was our "buy-in."

Well, I was never fooled. I used to say that if you really want my "buy-in," how about taking me to Vancouver Island with you? Contrast this with my experience in 1993, when we gathered together more than two hundred people from my department for a really big conversation. Everyone was there — from the receptionist to the Director General. We employed a modified OpenSpace technique. (OpenSpace is a large group systems-based tool that gathers together everyone in the system for a solution-based conversation). The theme of the session was, "To improve our effectiveness in the next twelve months we better pay attention to..." Over one hundred and twenty recommendations were generated from this energetic and thoughtful event. At the end of the session, the Director General announced that he would take those recommendations to a retreat on Vancouver Island three weeks hence. He did just that and, with the aid of a consultant and flip chart, drafted a new plan and returned, rested and tanned, to share it with us. Did he need our "buy-in" at that point? Of course not! We recognized all kinds of elements in the new plan from the earlier, large group session. We were "brought in" not "bought in."

I make no claims about understanding the ancient and fine art of leadership, but I will go back to the two fundamental ideas I mentioned in reference to our cave-dwelling ancestors. To lead others, you must be chosen by them, not impose yourself upon them. Once chosen, you must accept the mantle of leadership without also assuming you know it all.

The command-and-control model too often imposed leadership, and generally assumed that intelligence primarily exists at the top. In the new, knowledge-based world, leadership more than ever must be a reflection of the reality of those being led, and the leader must have a clear understanding of where intelligence resides, and how make full use of it.

I believe that one of the clearest examples of the required shift in thinking can be taken from a particularly bad habit we have seen in the public service. One way I distinguish leadership from management is through my assumption that leaders tend to be concerned with people, and managers tend to be concerned with programs. So let's say we have this brilliant plant entomologist. He loves bugs. Loves his work. One of the smartest guys in the laboratory. And we need a new manager of this department, so how about this guy? Well, he sure knows his stuff. George is flattered. Also means a raise. A raise not coming down the pipe as long as he just deals in bugs. So they work it out and George is the new manager.

At first he loves it, especially the new digs, but soon those pesky people start coming into the office. They come with ideas, problems, solutions, tears and anger. George is not quite prepared for this. These people are nuts. Where is the DDT? He wishes he had his bugs back.

Well, you get the picture.

So many boardrooms are filled with people who would rather be writing policy, dealing with the public or inventing new things.

It gets back to how we choose leaders and leaders accepting leadership...caveman stuff!

And finally, one last thought on this leadership business, grasshopper. I believe the toughest change for us to accept is that leadership comes from all levels. The leadership of a file clerk on an innovative project (say, to change how we file invoices), is as critical to organizational effectiveness as the leadership of an executive leading a review of fiscal policy.

There is evidence, reported by cultural anthropologists, from all over the world, that more isolated, indigenous, native populations and cultures have learned to accept that leadership comes from all quarters of the tribe.

Bureaucratically Incorrect

They were well aware that their community had leaders for war, leaders for the hunt and leaders for the spirit. I once heard a story about a Deputy Minister who apparently had become rather vexed over the issue of performance pay. So the story goes, there were a number of competencies in which his executives had to demonstrate extraordinary performance to qualify for their bonus. One of these competencies was leadership.

Every year these executives would cycle through his office, each of them performing a little song and dance routine for him about how well they had demonstrated leadership over the past twelve months.

It bored him.

One year, out of sheer exasperation, the Deputy Minister announced that no longer would their merit pay be based on their own leadership performance. It would now be based on how many leaders they had developed that year.

The change was dramatic. Now each executive made a presentation accompanied by all the members of their team in whom they had nurtured some leadership ability during the past year. "Hey Deputy, this is Mary. With my support Mary assumed responsibility for a complete review of our ministerial briefing process and under her leadership the whole process has improved dramatically.

I have a friend, Paul Lefebvre, who is a professional management coach. He brings a novel perspective and clear vision for helping managers monitor their own performance. He also is a pioneer in the effort to bring coaching into the broader culture of the workplace, not just to the executives in need. He has proposed that on one day of the year, let's say April 1st, everyone in the organization gets to work for the manager of their choice, just for that day. Can you imagine the interesting scenarios that might develop if everyone went off to work for someone they really wanted to work with? It could turn out that some work areas could end up a little short.

Leadership, it appears, is best when it is both universal and personal.

9 • Communication

THE OTHER DAY, AN ARTICLE IN *The Globe and Mail* caught my eye. It seems that after two fruitless years of chasing leads on a string of unsolved, but apparently related homicides in British Columbia, a number of the local police departments finally met in person to compare notes. Within days, things began to heat up, the investigation started to coalesce, and suspects were being sought.

Well, duh...to quote that great social critic, Homer Simpson. To most of us it would seem the most natural thing we would do: talk to one another.

You want to know something, my young friend? I want to make a small wager with you. Over the next decade of your public service career, you will encounter many men and women who, like me, are involved in leadership and organizational change. We will come into your workspace with our markers and flip charts, trying to get a handle on what is bugging you and your colleagues. You probably already know the issue you and your workmates will rank number one on that chart-covered wall. Of course you do. Communication.

Communication, communication, communication.

We hear it all the time. If we find more money to spend, we may get another contract to undertake yet another communications study, or perhaps produce one more interminable communications plan. Oh boy, are we getting good at studying communication, talking about communication and planning communication strategies. We find the time and the money to do all of this. However, we don't seem to have the time to talk to one another.

I recall presenting a session at a seminar some years ago. I launched into my usual rant about boardroom tables and how they tend to obfuscate conversation. After my session, a huge, burly, bearded man came up to me, shook my hand and suggested that, indeed, he had the same problem. Even when I take my management team on retreats," he said, "I cannot seem to wean them from a board table. Just once I would like us to step away from the table, sit together in a circle of comfortable chairs, and have a real conversation about our business."

"And what is your business?" I inquired.

"I am a vice president in charge of creative development for the Disney Corporation," he replied.

"Good grief," I choked, "you are working for Mickey Mouse and you still can't loosen up?" If he has a problem, then what am I going to do, I thought, with a bunch of managers at a retreat looking at the impact of the spruce budworm on the sub boreal ecosystem?

It's not that today's public servants don't try to communicate. The problem is, we practice what I call "managed communication." We have meetings, committees and workshops instead of conversations. These events teach us to communicate "key messages" and "talking points." We overuse the communication colossus PowerPoint instead of engaging in the old-fashioned, straight-from-the-heart art of conversation. We hold town-hall forums with citizens, but they become free-for-alls for the discharge of frustration by all those citizens lined up at the microphone. Communication at these events involves us making speeches and presentations to the audience-usually made up of the citizens. This is followed by those same people making speeches back at us. To regain trust with citizens, we are going to have to find and use tools that allow us to tank the speeches and return to conversation.

We really are quite messed up with this one, grasshopper. You see, as with other issues in the workplace, it comes back to the element of risk.

It is risky to have a real conversation. Just ask the one you love. In conversation, we can show passion. In conversation, our depth of real knowledge is exposed. In conversation, we could be wrong. With managed communication, we can eliminate these potential irritants and risks.

The beauty of conversation is that we generally go deeper than any presentation. In conversation, the knowledge is spread around and shared, and therefore not limited. In conversation, being wrong is not an indictable offence, because in conversation, you are not putting forward your information and ideas as irrefutable truth.

Go back, for a moment, to those police forces in British Columbia. My guess is that they had "open communication" throughout, from day one. They probably sent memos, exchanged requests and maybe had some meetings. My guess is that the real breakthrough came when they stopped swapping information and positions, and started having real conversations about what they knew and what they did not know.

I find it sadly ironic that in the public service, we are terrified of those we serve...the public.

If I had a quarter for every public service manager I have heard mutter, "The public is going to kill us on this if they find out," I would never need to buy a retirement dream lottery ticket again.

I believe the public is neither scary nor stupid. There have been so many issues in the last few decades that have put public service and individual public servants on the front page of *The Globe and Mail*. So what? It is important for those issues to be broadcast in the press. Yet for the most part, we duck and weave — if not to cover up actual scandals — in the hope of not incurring the wrath of the citizen.

Not long ago, I was interested to observe that it took a cornered politician to show us how the public really reacts to an open conversation. When a drunken, obnoxious premier selected a group of homeless men and took a shot at them, the effort backfired, and he found himself with two options: bring in the communications management experts and spin it out as best you can, or play it out in real conversation.

Ralph Klein played it out. You can only imagine the subsequent conversations he must have had with his family, caucus and colleagues. But we got to watch his conversations with the public. Cynics may have seen a man struggling to get out of a jam, but I saw a man who recognized an opportunity to have a real conversation about what he had to do.

And he pulled it off.

To be successful in moving an organization from a culture of managed communication to the more open culture of conversation, we will require new tools and processes.

Bureaucratically Incorrect

We are excited about the possibilities opening up for systems communication using tools such as the modified Open Space, the Courtyard Café, the Standup and the Talk Show as alternatives to anaemic meetings and town-hall consultations. The power of conversation cuts through the terminally stupefying drone of presentations, speechifying and positioning.

In a world where it is still acceptable to learn to crawl before walking, we need to practice these and other new tools. We need to begin building receptivity in our colleagues to the emerging world of workplace conversation.

At the same time we must have a greater vision. This is the time to go back and re-read the writings of David Bohm and his acolyte, William Isaacs. Bohm, you will recall, was a contemporary of Albert Einstein. He became discouraged with the world of physics after bumping up against the worst of the McCarthy era. He decided to devote the rest of his life to the study of dialogue. Dialogue, if you will, is the cognac of conversation. Simply put, dialogue is a way for people to inquire together through focused conversation. It differs from discussion (a word which comes from the same root as percussion and concussion) wherein people tend to bounce ideas around and perhaps even try to score points. Dialogue comes from the Greek dia-logos with dia meaning word and logos meaning through. Dialogue is much more the flow of meaning through a group of people. Four essential practices include *voicing*: speaking your authentic voice, *listening*: deeply without resistance, *respecting*: yourself and others integrity of position and *suspending*: stepping back from your deeply held assumptions and certainties. Dialogue requires time, skilled moderation and long term commitment. It is not for quick decision-making and immediate action.

Bohm believed dialogue would crack the back of strife in Northern Ireland, the Middle East and other hotbeds of hatred around the world. We will see. Already we hear reports of dialogue having worked successfully in labour disputes in the steel mills of the southern United States. We are already seeing the emerging dialogue practice in our own public service by colleagues such as Catherine Auger of Health Canada.

Just like the learning continuum of data, information, and knowledge and finally wisdom, there's a continuum of speech, communication, conversation and finally, dialogue. Tough stuff to get your head around, learn about and — most of all — practice.

In the service of the public, however, we ignore it at our peril.

10 • Change

*E*VERYTHING IS ABOUT CHANGE. Geopolitics, the environment, the economy, shifting political and social realities — and, of course, our organization's response to all of them — reflects the fact that we live and work in constant change.

Human beings have been adapting to change since the beginning of time, even though we tend to believe change was slower and easier in earlier times. I would imagine however, those humans have always feared and resisted change no matter how fast it may be happening. The Industrial/ Scientific Age, however, gave us the conceit we could now deal with change in a more scientific or thoughtful way. Perhaps we could control change more than it controlled us. This was the core thinking behind the work of Frederick Taylor, the godfather of early change management. His work is now referred to as Scientific Management, and vestiges of some of his ideas and practices continue to influence our workplace.

Taylor studied the impact of the Industrial Revolution on the workplace. Before the Industrial Revolution, we lived in the Age of Craft, a time when the ordinary labourer did it all. A potter dug his clay, mixed it, formed it into vessels, decorated and then fired them in a high-temperature kiln. He would then take the finished pieces to the local market and sell them.

Taylor looked at this process and found it cumbersome, slow and very inefficient for the emerging changes and challenges of industrial production. Efficiency, he believed, would come by breaking up the production process into little steps or stages, training a person in every possible detail of their step or stage, then implementing all of the steps in sequence to reassemble the whole process. The modern assembly-line process stands as the ultimate tool and legacy of Scientific Management.

Remember that this sort of process relies on a top-down, command-and-control style of management. Though we talked of this before, we didn't dwell on how this type of management cuts the worker out of the thinking process. Now, Taylor was right when he realized that most potters had limitations. Some were good at producing strong forms but weak when it came to the decoration. Others were lacking in marketing skills.

In breaking up the manufacturing and marketing process — into a series of stages — the wholeness experienced by the individual worker got lost in the shuffle. Workers could only see and toil on their allotted piece of the process. A traditional potter knew pots. Every day, they learned something new about some aspect of the process as a whole. The efficiency-based command-and-control model created a new mental model for potters, buggy makers and farmers. They had been autonomous individuals — creator, manufacturer, marketer — accustomed to being intimately involved with the whole process. This required that they tap into their whole brain capacity to think things through and problem-solve for themselves, rather than having someone else think it through for them as dictated by the new scientific model.

So, Scientific Management increased productivity; it got the goods out...lots of them, fast! But it also produced the legacy of a dehumanized, mechanistic and sometimes angry workforce. Change became autocratic, something that was imposed from above and thought-through by only those few people at the top. Consequently, it required a tougher form of management, which of course was met with more anger and resistance from those responsible for the production, the emerging labour movement.

The legacy of Scientific Management remains to this day, and while things have changed, the scent of its decay, from all those years of distrust and misery lingers in many places of work in both the public and private-sector.

One of the more positive results of the Scientific Management backlash was a new school of studies in human relations, and the application of new social and psychological theories in the workplace. Just as Taylor's work emphasized the technical side of science as an antidote to inefficiency, turn of the century social theorists like Kurt Lewin and Douglas McGregor looked to the new field of social science for inspiration. They began to study human

Bureaucratically Incorrect

as well as technical aspects in their management models. In his fine book, *Productive Workplaces*, Weisbord references Taylor as suggesting, "The general adoption of Scientific Management would readily double the future productivity of the average man in industrial work." Years later, McGregor would assert, "Many managers would agree that the effectiveness of their organizations would be at least doubled if they could discover how to tap the unrealized potential present in their human resources." One approach promises double the productivity through process, the other through people.

This represented a major shift in mental models of organizational change. Agents for change in the workplace began to see the human relations dynamic as the critical and possibly the ultimate, most successful approach to humanizing the workplace. In focusing on human relations issues, this mental model essentially led to the following assumption: in order to change organizations, you first had to change the people. This is a noble idea, but also fraught with a several concerns.

I can remember attending a workshop in 1973 presented by some idiot who received a lot of money to hold sixty of us hostage in a room. He yelled at us, berated us and exhorted us to fight back and get in touch with our gut feelings. I wanted to give him a brand new feeling in his gut, but that would have led to litigation. Some people yelled back, left the session early or broke down in tears. The facilitator may have felt like he had made a breakthrough with some of us, but he should have been in our office the following week. Not only did we have our continuing dysfunctional system to deal with, all of us in attendance were also really annoyed with our department for hiring this jerk to confirm things which we already knew.

It is my own opinion, grasshopper, that change management has been managed, influenced and perhaps even controlled by the theorists — those from the behavioural sciences and human relations schools of thought — and that this has been going on for decades and continues to this day.

I last attended a change workshop a few years ago. I went full of high hopes, expecting great things. The whole day involved modified New Age, feel-good exercises, from listening to jazz lite in the dark while writing ten things we loved about ourselves, to using a crystal on our desk as a means of identifying "bad energy" in other people.

Bureaucratically Incorrect

Let's take a breath here for a minute. Some of this personal, transformation stuff is really good for you. Great, even. People crave personal transformation and why not? It is a form of change and, arguably, changed people make better workplace colleagues. No problem there.

I am just not sure how much we should be paying for it, and whether it is a critical priority for change management, especially during times of reduced budgets, which might, perhaps, be better spent in changing the system as well as the people within it!

I am no expert in learning organization theory, but the more I read and the more I try to practice, the more I find that real change in organizations is most effective when it is structural change. We have talked about this before. People are not idiots by nature. They often get a little crazy by working in poorly designed systems. Structure a system with too much red tape, bottlenecks, poor decision-making, lack of participation and other assorted structural limitations, and people soon start going to pieces. Go ahead; send them off on a personal transformation experience or a stress management seminar or an anger management workshop.

They will come back to work feeling much better, thank you very much. But two or three days later, back in the world of hurt, red tape, bottlenecks, etc., guess what? They will be behaving like idiots again.

It is my sincere belief that we are going to have to transform our organizations into the kind of workplaces that strive to cut the red tape, unplug the bottlenecks, speed up and achieve more effective decision-making and widen opportunities for participation on a daily basis. If we do this in a spirit of accountability and due diligence, then, one day, we may suddenly be pleasantly surprised over the extent of our own, and other's, transformation.

So my friend, I encourage you to seek out you own personal transformation. There are more books in big box bookstores and more workshops available in your community than you can shake a stick at. Go for it if you must. Personally, I would recommend taking up jazz guitar, or learning how to climb a rock face or volunteering at a food bank as a better approach to finding personal transformation, than allocating corporate time and money on another personal growth workshop for the team.

Bureaucratically Incorrect

In fact, I wonder how many workshops would be at risk of cancellation for lack of participation if employees had to pay for their own attendance.

On the other hand, if you find yourself in a setting where you learn something about yourself (be it during a university course, or a great seminar), keep it; you paid for it! As for organizations, we must be diligent in our insistence that we do our best to fix the system before we try to fix the people.

11 • Innovation

A WHILE BACK I HEARD AN EXCITING INTERVIEW on CBC Radio. The piece was all about the advent of a new approach to emergency response in the West End of London, England — bicycles!

When a 911 call comes in, the first response is now a paramedic on a bicycle, followed by an ambulance.

The young man being interviewed was the innovator. He was a BMX and mountain bike champion who worked as a paramedic to support his habit. One day while thinking aloud, he bet with himself that he could outpace the ambulance on his bike in West End London traffic. He could, and he did.

Apparently, his managers were impressed, because he has just finished training a team of six bicycle paramedics who zip through the traffic and crowds with life support paraphernalia tucked into their panniers. The ambulances trail behind as best they can.

Innovation! I grew up in a public service that experienced a truly innovative idea perhaps once every three or four years — if we were lucky. Worse, as innovative ideas were presented, a culture of fear, jealousy and self-interest drove them back. In many public sector organizations, innovation was considered serendipitous at best and seditious at worst. Sometimes innovation is simply stopped in its tracks by the lethargy of bureaucratic decision making. A while back, I had a conversation with a physician who told me how he had managed to secure funding and support for computers, technical equipment and everything else but the space, for an innovative diabetes clinic in a small city. For more than two years, he and his colleagues have sat on this money, waiting for space to be provided to run this innovative clinic. The administrative bureaucracy solely concerned about space allocation, has yet to get around to finding them a spot. Though this doctor spent considerable time and effort to secure resources for an innovative project, after all the delay he was getting ready to send the money back to the sponsors and deep-six the whole thing. Two years!

The public sector of the future must be prepared to embrace innovation — as it is learning to do with change. Let's stop here for a minute and make sure we understand the difference between innovation and change. We know that we live in a state of constant change. Change, however, comes for many different reasons. Change can be imposed from the outside, as in changes in government and ministers. Change can come from large-scale events such as September 11th. Change can come with a new boss who wants to make a mark. The impact of change can be positive or negative, depending on the initiator, the response and the results.

Take September 11th, for example. Many public service agencies' response was to close down projects and return to older, more established ways of doing business. Others, out of necessity and empowered thinking, started generating some really creative ideas. An example of this is the border pass card, so popular with car drivers that it is now being used by the trucking industry. That's innovation!

You can read a lot of books and listen to a lot of speakers on the subject of innovation and change. Change is constant. Innovation or a traditional response to change is optional. We can get so caught up managing change, that we lose focus on managing our daily work. Let's take a look at this with a more practical example.

A subject near and dear to your heart and mine is the latest effort to pay more attention to shifting demographics in the workplace. The big issue, in particular, is the reality of boomers like me leaving the public service, creating an urgent need to recruit and retain youth like yourself.

Fair enough. It is a good plan.

So what actually happens? Well, in typical big-organization style, we think that because this is a big change, we must need big posters, big marketing and big conferences.

In the meantime, I am thinking of someone named Sarah, although I am not sure if that was her name. I was sitting beside her at some function and, as is my fashion, I started to ask questions. She was twenty-three years old and eighteen months into her career as a public servant. So I zeroed in on her state of mind: "What are two things that have driven you crazy since you joined the public service?"

"You really want to know?" she replied.

I did.

So she began. She told me the story of how she was sent out to a community to promote a new initiative. In her conversation with a young local official, she got the brush-off. "Oh, it's just another government boondoggle," he laughed.

"No, no," she insisted, "this is really going to work; it's a great concept." Finally, he agreed to have her send out material that could get them started as a pilot project.

She went back to the office and immediately put a package together and started to type a cover letter. A colleague noticed, stopped her and said, "You can't write that letter. It has to go out under our supervisor's authority."

Okay. She took the work to the supervisor, who promised to look after it.

A couple of days later, she inquired about the status and was informed that the supervisor could not write the letter either, and everything had been forwarded up to the manager.

Well, to cut to the finish, two weeks later, the package remained sitting on someone's desk. Sarah looked me in the eye and said, "You know, right now that guy in the community has even more ammunition behind his belief that we don't deliver in government."

There was a second issue as well. Turns out Sarah had dispatched a letter that contained an error in fact. Her boss called her in, pointed out the mistake and apologized to Sarah for not catching it when it came up to her desk. That made Sarah truly furious. "Why did she need to accept responsibility for not catching my mistake? She won't even let me take responsibility for my own screw-ups? Not only am I not really granted the responsibility to do the job, it's as if — anytime I mess up — I'm not expected to take responsibility for that either."

I don't really think young people want to be seen as some sort token nod to innovation. Hiring young people is not an innovation strategy. I think they want to be seen as part of the solution to ongoing change. They want to feel like their innovative ideas will be heard.

It may suit our strategic goals to establish a high profile recruitment and retention process, and do that with lots of meetings and printed materials. But in the meantime, all our new recruits really want is the opportunity to do a good job...a really good job.

And by the way, this is where I think innovation really kicks in. Innovation is not change. Innovation is the fuel of planned, thoughtful, positive and continuous improvement, based on our response to change.

Innovation is not just eureka moments. Innovation can be slow and even plodding. Innovation can be cultural. Innovation can be strategic. Innovation can be what you do every day.

If we really want to attract and keep young people in public service, then perhaps, instead of organizing a conference once in a while, we should give them innovative challenges...every day.

Hey you....

• find me a better way to track these invoices…
• think of some unique ways to get parental input into these children's school day…
• look into some spicier ways to run this new set of town hall meetings…

You can ask for innovation; you don't have to wait for it to happen. But please don't ask for it if you won't listen to what you may hear with an open mind and a willingness to follow through.

Innovation is the cheesecake in a meat-and-potatoes work world. Innovation is where a lot of the attraction to work lives.

We often steal people's cheesecake. It's not a good way to recruit and retain.

12 • Social Graces

Social Graces...how did that get in here? I am not sure but I feel a strong compulsion these days to go there. Have you watched question period lately, walked through a mall or taken a ride on a city bus? The lost art of practicing good social graces it appears, is still in decline. The workplace is not immune to this slippery slope. I will go out on a limb here and suggest that, should we by some miracle, bring an improvement in social graces back into the workplace, we could possibly eliminate sixty to seventy per cent of our human relations issues. I suppose that there were no better manners practiced when I was a young public servant. In fact, it may have been my cohort that gave general etiquette the big kiss-off. Well, we were just blowing smoke in those days (perhaps that was part of the problem), and we are sorry. Could you please find it in your hearts to try and find some of that etiquette and put it back where it belongs?

The last bastion of social graces in public service may be with our colleagues in uniform. If you talk to an old hand in the RCMP like Sergeant Major Hugh Stewart, whose seniority and rank now give him responsibility for protocol on the west coast, he becomes quite animated about the subject. Even when members of the tactical team, his specialty, are out in tents in the snow, sleeping in an abandoned building or in some other god-forsaken circumstance, early light will see them rising in the dark with the first item of the day, troop call. They greet one another at the start of each day with both camaraderie and respect.

When they have a special event in the mess, they set aside rank and call each other Mr. or Ms. It's a way of acknowledging their comradeship. Before starting, they toast Her Majesty, the Force and their fallen comrades. You learn manners in a mess. Talk to someone like Bob Thompson, who is a

Lieutenant Commander in the Navy. We shared a great conversation initiated over an old Navy book on etiquette. Bob Thompson credits that history of everyday courtesy with the continued character building that is still required in a highly effective military team.

I am not suggesting for a minute that we start toasting the Queen on the third floor in the Ministry of Finance in British Columbia. And I know you are not going to find many pages on social graces in professional management books. I don't really care. If you wanted a book strictly about professional management stuff, you wasted your money on this one! And so, pressing on, I am more than determined to have a chat with you about the importance of improving social graces in the workplace.

It seems so old-fashioned. Even the word has a quality to it that implies a bygone era. As a person who lived through the tail end of those times, I admit that I am content to see the demise of a completely manners-driven society.

For the most part, manners were rule-based, just like some of our organizations. They reflected an older, deeper connection to a more class-based society. Manners were considered to reflect good breeding (we actually talked like that), wealth and education. Manners helped prop up stupid ideas like the inequality of the sexes. The world of manners needed a swift kick, and essentially got it.

But like the proverbial baby and the bath water, we may have lost more than we anticipated. So now we have no rules, no equality and no class.

Well, not really. The contemporary workplace has been developing a few new rules, good ones, but these are usually related to big issues like harassment and abusive behaviour. While we seem to accept the idea of equality of opportunity for the sexes, both sides could still work on some of the basics of common courtesy. While no one wants to return to the old class distinctions, when was the last time you saw a smart, well-dressed public servant, bright-eyed and full of healthful vigour, skip briskly up a flight of steps, looking for a hand to shake, and bursting at the seams to do good? I agree that it is an odd image, but not without some charm.

As a kid, I remember such characters. They were public servants in uniform, in suits and in style. My mother would comment, "There goes Mr. Pleasance, the town clerk." He would tip his hat and say hello.

I feel your nervousness already with my references to dress. Lighten up. It's not that critical, but we will be getting back to it later.

More importantly, these people had a basic etiquette. They had manners for two reasons. First, they were raised having learned some common courtesy and, like DNA, manners were simply an integral part of their personality. Second, as public servants, they represented the government, and a government that did not show respect for a citizen was not a government to be trusted.

So it's not 1954; it's 2004. What do we want fifty years later? I just think we need to have some more conversations about the role of social graces in the workplace. I believe that most public servants do exercise basic courtesy with the public and our partners, but there is always room for improvement. I am really more interested in our manners with each other.

Social graces seem to break down quickly and with the greatest detrimental effect on those closest to us. Families decry the lack of manners in the home. Sometimes, we take those we love for granted and do the most stupid of things without thinking.

It is likewise with our colleagues. We can and sometimes do take each other for granted. I remember coming up with the idea for an early morning Standup session on our team. I was frustrated by the fact that team members didn't always exchange hellos before starting another day's work. It seems crazy to think of it, but day after day people came to work, said hello to people they passed on their way to their cubicle, then tucked into their work without truly acknowledging their team members.

We take each other for granted.

We shout out "howya doin!" but don't really expect an answer or even wait long enough to see if one is forthcoming. It's so insincere! The thought of looking into a co-worker's eyes and asking about his kid, spouse or health — old-time etiquette stuff — feels a little too messy these days.

Heck, she might even answer back, and then what would happen?

We squabble over who gets the coffee for the meeting, instead of delighting in serving our fellow workers.

We don't always take that newcomer around the office and introduce her to everyone. It will happen sooner or later, we figure, and anyway isn't that supposed to be done by someone from Human Resources? As for the use of please and thank-you in the hundreds of daily requests and promises, don't even start.

I had a boss who actually sent out thank-you notes to people after they did a particularly good job on something. I would love to be the recipient of such a card or note today!

So, okay, let's get back to that dress business.

I know it makes you nervous. It makes me anxious as well. I am one of the original dress-down guys. I was determined to never become one of those stuffy suit-and-tie people. Jeans in the office? I may have started that trend. I am here because I do good work, not for how I look was my attitude.

Well, I take it back. I am sorry for all those years that colleagues had to see me every morning in bland, boring, rumpled Harris Tweed sport coats and faded blue jeans. I now know these clothes contributed to my similarly over-casual approach to writing, speaking, thinking and decision-making.

So, I don't want to go back to dress codes. That can become a top-down-rules thing again. But I do feel strongly, grasshopper, that you feel better if you look better.

As an antidote to "dress down Friday's," I propose we implement "dress up Monday's." Crisp suits, polished shoes and ironed T-shirts for all!

So, in the big picture, this social graces stuff is a pretty small item on the big corporate agenda, but I am glad that I was able to bring it to your attention.

It occurs to me that there are so many big issues in today's workplace. Gender equality, diversity, harassment and work/life balance are a few of the issues that dominate our organizational concerns. And so they should.

Still, we might want to consider starting with something somewhat smaller and more manageable, and get a result!

When Rudy Giuliani decided to clean up New York, he wisely decided to start small. Using the "broken windows" theory, he went after the turnstile jumpers, the jaywalkers and the graffiti sprayers. Within a few years, the murder rate, robbery rates and violent crime statistics started to drop. New York hit the "tipping point" by succeeding with the small stuff first.

Your generation coined the phrase, "Think globally, and act locally." In organizations, it just may be that the tiny but important impact of renewing those small social graces could lead to even better success in tackling those big-ticket items like harassment, etc. down the road.

Bureaucratically Incorrect

13 • Rewards

I HAVE SAID THIS BEFORE, BUT IT BEARS REPEATING. If I am awarded one more coffee mug, I am going to start smoking again. I know it sounds a bit harsh, but I really need a lot more of a reward than a mug if I am doing a good job. I want the really big prize...the pat on the back!

I recall an early lesson. There was a period when, as a struggling student, I needed just one more class to qualify as a special education teacher in northern Manitoba. Along with my wife and our two kids, (one sleeping in a banana box, since there were no child car seats in those days) we packed up our battered '53 Plymouth and lit out for Winnipeg to take a summer-school course in child psychology. Lacking money for rent, we lived in a campground on the edge of the city and slept in a leaky tent. The course was in applied psychology and provided an overview of special needs children. My previous studies had already led me into the uncertain world of psychology and, with an appreciation for Maslow's hierarchy of needs, I felt far more comfortable with the warm ideas of that master of client-centred warmth, Carl Rogers.

It was 1968, so of course I bought into the whole Rogerian package. In fact, I got so good at it that students from a class down the hall — one focused on the nasty Skinnerian approach — would come and fetch me out of class to help them argue against the horrible views of their professor, who was deeply into espousing the "evils" of behaviour-modification.

One day their professor was well into the swing of his lecture which involved a story about his helping a grade-five boy raise his grade from a D to a B. He had devised and presented to the boy's distraught mother, a behavioural modification plan that involved cash incentives which were to be doled out at critical steps. In six months, the boy's improvement was outstanding.

I jumped up in great indignation and, in the spirit of those non-materialistic times, argued against the morality and validity of using money to influence a child to change his behaviour.

"You don't like the money idea?" the professor responded.

"Not for a minute," I lipped back self-righteously.

"Then use hugs and kisses," he retorted.

Ouch, he had a point! I was beat! To this day, I cannot see the world of human relationships in such narrow Skinnerian or, indeed, Rogerian terms. But, I have seen the power of hugs, kisses, kind words and pats on the back as they cut through the psychobabble and give people the strength to do better and feel better about whom they are and what they do.

This year, I met an interesting young public servant on Vancouver Island. We were building a community of practice in learning organizations and, as is our custom, we were taking extra time to hear everyone's story.

Dan's story was not at all typical. He was born into a successful middle-class family. Raised to seek out challenges, he became a young actor and was earning six figures at the tender age of eighteen in a television series. When the series tanked, he took a job as a teamster on the Vancouver docks. It was a completely different world — rough would be an understatement. There were bosses on the take, goods falling off trucks and the constant presence of biker gangs. He noticed things. For example, there seemed to be a lot of things falling off the trucks, so to speak. What is going on? he asks with youthful naiveté. "You guys got something going on here?"

Well, they took him aside, straightened him around and asked him a few choice questions. He was, of course, a really bright kid and they liked his answers. Soon they were courting him, swelling his head with how smart he was and how they could use a smart guy like him. He ate it up. He did really well at his new work.

A year later he was in a Washington State jail.

The good news is that he got out straightened out, went back to school, eventually earned an MBA and sharpened up the true mind for business he always had.

Here was the interesting part for me. Over a beer that night, he lamented how incredibly proficient the bad guys are at making young people feel special. They can spot talent, smarts and attitude from a long way off and they move in, recruit and promote that person from the very beginning.

Today in the public sector, Dan observes that managers, clients and even co-workers send out different signals when a young bright person shows their stuff. They sometimes signal a bit of jealousy, they may respond to ideas negatively and often they imply that by recruiting this person we somehow brought inconvenience into their lives.

Bob, he asked me, how come the bad guys know enough to stroke your ego, make you feel special and send signals that they want to invest in you and make you part of the gang? Faster than you can imagine, they have you connected, hooked up to the right people and provided the resources you need to succeed, all the while making you feel good about yourself, making you feel that you belong.

But the good guys, he implied, give out those same rewards like candy at Christmas, once a year and only because they have to.

Frankly, he gave me a lot to think about that evening. Why do the bad guys have such great reward and recognition programs? Sure, they give out money, but all the money in the world wouldn't get most of us into a biker gang. You have to be recruited in a much deeper way. First, you have to be seen as smart, creative, brave or whatever — something they want; something they need. Then they reward everything you do with the equivalent of that pat on the back.

In our organizations, I seldom hear people tell stories of how they were spotted, praised, recruited and kept on the team through constant positive reinforcement.

Oh sure, we recognize that we don't do a great job of reward and recognition. We pay people big dollars to tell us that. So what do we do? Well, first we study the problem. Then we design and create a new reward and recognition program. You know how we love the programs.

Somehow, I don't see a biker gang paying a consultant to come and study their reward and recognition practices. And I cannot even imagine an Employee of the Month poster in the clubhouse.

Dan tells me the bikers have a culture that makes you feel good about belonging to something bad. Why can we not create a culture that makes us feel good about belonging to something that also does good?

We old folks sometimes get a little mixed up about things. We think you should be happy just to be here, to have a job. We think that, heck, if we are miserable, then you should be, too. We think that your knowing something we don't is a threat to us, to our position and our history.

And of course if all else fails, don't those people in human resources have some kind of program to look after all this stuff?

So, help us out a little here if you don't mind. If you are already using good tools like the Standup every morning, make sure that each day, you pat someone on the back in Standup. Trust me; you will begin to infect the system, and soon you may even get reciprocal recompense.

Recruit people. Let smart people know how much you would like it if they were a part of your team. Look for people who need a shot of praise. Then shoot them. No more mugs. Going for coffee with the right person is much better. Turn in your mugs and ask to be taken out for coffee and a good word instead.

14 • Ethics

THE OTHER DAY, SOMEONE ASKED ME ABOUT THE ISSUE OF ETHICS and what exactly is the big deal with ethics and values in the public service today. Well, let me suggest that perhaps we are moving into interesting territory with ethics.

Every so often, we witness or hear about a cabinet minister coming under fire for questionable contracts or perhaps an ADM taking a warm weather junket inappropriately funded through a client's office. The news wires heat up, denials spin out and the communications people on the eighth floor work overtime.

Inevitably, in the ensuing chaos, we hear the word "ethics" brought up — as in the lack of, the enforcement of, or the oversight of.

Ethics are principles we act on by choice, and they help us to determine what is right and wrong in whatever context or set of circumstances we find ourselves. Ethics are as old as human beings. No doubt ethical considerations played a part in cave banishments. As we developed as a species, we tended to find a home for ethics in the spiritual world. Modernity brought philosophy and a more philosophical approach to ethics and ethical behaviour. Traditionally, the rather passive teaching of ethics has been left up to the family, community and then the formal process of education to address.

Ethics in the public sector workplace has a long and honorable history. Ethics were initially developed according to codes of practice. Physicians used the Hippocratic Oath as early as 350 B.C. Teachers and other professional groups got together in associations. Guilds for craftsmen and women with a clearly defined set of skills (e.g., silversmithing) developed their own codes of conduct.

The longevity of the conversation around ethics in which professionals have indulged has contributed to a strong foundation, but there are cracks and shaky supports in that model as well. By tying ethics perhaps too narrowly to the professional groups, we run the risk of overlooking the importance of ethical behaviour and ethical considerations for everyone else. The manual labourers, the skilled and semi-skilled and the paraprofessionals in the workplace and world of work and, even more importantly, those we serve — our customers, clients and citizens also benefit by working to a code of ethics.

As an example, if ethical behaviour was something expected only of those with professional education and training, a hospital would rely on the medical association, nurses associations, and public administration associations and so on, to manage ethical issues. In reality, the primary concern of a hospital is patient care. To succeed in providing the best of patient care, ethical behaviour must be seen as the responsibility of the entire hospital — from the discreet conduct of the janitor, working on the floor of a ward, to the fiscal accountability of the CFO.

The notion of looking at ethics holistically within a systems framework is relatively recent, but it is an approach that is fast gaining in popularity.

As public service organizations improve, they are realizing that they cannot function without a vision or mission. They also cannot function without a corporate sense of principles, values and ethical conduct.

The work of the late John Tait on ethics in the federal public service is a fine benchmark. It describes the unique qualities of ethical behaviour in public service, and I encourage you to read the full report. Tait saw ethics in relation to six particular areas.

He begins with the very important democratic context, and the challenge of accountability. He describes the evolving accountability push-and-pull between the minister and public servant, new models of service delivery (i.e., agencies) and the tension between political and public service values. He refers to "speaking truth to power" which means that everyone must feel comfortable in speaking up to the boss. This is an important consideration in these days of "whistle blowing."

In referring to employment and values, he describes security of tenure, always a topic of great and frequent discussion. My generation actually believed if they worked hard, stayed on the job and didn't kill anyone in the workplace, they would "retire in harness," as they liked to say. The great downsizing effort curtailed that notion pretty fast. It appears that loyalty from your generation is still expected, but it is not tied to the same reward of tenure. Employees are expected to work for the public good, not for self-advantage. In return, employers support the employee by practicing good leadership and people-management policies.

I particularly like Tait's discussion of a critical mass of values. When a new employee, like yourself, comes in, do you immediately sense that you are in the company of a large group of public sector professionals who demonstrate a clearly defined set workplace values? If you feel it, then it's not because there is a list on the wall but because those values constitute a critical mass in the culture.

Tait's third area of concern relates to the principles of public service. I do not believe Tait wanted simply to establish a glowing list of core public-service values. Rather, in a much more fundamental way, he wanted us to propagate a continuing conversation in our workplace that encouraged these values to emerge in dialogue and play out in practice. He envisioned four families, if you will, of public service values.

Democratic values that would include concepts such as responsible government, rule of law, support for democracy, due process and accountability. *Traditional professional values* would be those like neutrality, merit, excellence and speaking truth to power. New professional values might include innovation, creativity, collaboration and teamwork. *Ethical values* included more traditional, positive behavioural values such as integrity, honesty, equity and discretion.

The fourth family of values revolved around *value for people* — customers, clients, and citizens — and included such things as respect, tolerance, caring, decency and courage.

Can values change? We know those policies, practices and programs are in a constant state of flux. For the most part, we consider these to be open to change as long as they are firmly grounded with a clear set of ethical principles and values. However, we must be aware that values do shift sometimes in our society. They have done so historically, and will continue

(right margin, handwritten/stylized) Bureaucratically Incorrect

to evolve. Think just for a minute about the shift in values over the past thirty years around gender, sexuality, birth, death and diversity. Values are not rigid; they shift and evolve as well.

In his fourth area of concern, Tait asks us to consider what happens when values collide. For example, what happens when the traditional values of public administration (top-down, regulations, and ministerial prerogative) are challenged by public-management perspective (leadership, client satisfaction, new work methods)?

We must acknowledge that, as your generation works towards new ways of doing the job, you are challenging not only the methods of work, but also the underlying values driving the culture and nature of the workplace. At the same time new ideas are not necessarily better and we still want to adhere and have great respect for the older, foundational values.

I missed this. In my tenure as a public servant, there was never any conversation around underlying values. The discussion was always about the surface stuff. It was always about this program versus that program, instead of developing a deeper understanding through dialogue about why we were even doing something.

Tait's fifth area of concern asks us square on, what is our choice when values are in conflict? He is clear that, in some cases, there is no choice. Examples where there is little or no choice could include the Conflict of Interest Guidelines and the Post Employment Code. But as everything changes, we find more and more, that ethical distinctions are being clarified, confronted and resolved by public service employees who are closer to the front line of service.

Sometimes, I often think it was easier the old way. No responsibility; just follow rules and guidelines. They protected you and gave the system its accountability. They also choked real effectiveness, creativity and innovation.

If we want to reduce the monolithic imposition of ethics and make ethics real and flexible at the local level, we must personalize accountability and start to build it into our front line work. Not only will this empower us as public servants and bring us new benefits, but also it will encourage the development and growth of a corresponding responsibility among and in those we serve.

Bureaucratically Incorrect

In his sixth area of concern, Tait asks us to look at leadership and values. Although we've discussed leadership already, it's time to go there again because I consider it to be at the core of both values and ethics.

"Managers administer programs, leaders lead people" is a rather simplistic statement. Yet, when we look at values and ethics, we understand that they do not reside in programs and policies. They reside within people. Therefore, we require an approach to leadership that models values, supports values and works to values. If there is a leadership disconnect where values are espoused but not lived, cynicism will grow like moss on a West Coast condo.

Once again, I urge you to seek out Tait's work.

I want to leave you, however, with some basic thoughts about all this values and ethics stuff. These past couple of decades, I've observed those in management trying to come to grips with one of the first and most fundamental tenets of learning organizations, which is, that learning organizations must be led by shared vision and values.

Our response to these ideas has always been one of compliance. You want a mission statement? Okay, let's hire some help, pick a group of people to go on a retreat and have them craft a mission statement. When they come back, we will get the communications people to knock the passion out of it and we will get it in place and on the wall. Ten years later, we decide we need to identify our values. No problem! Get another group, send them off and back they come with a fine list of values to go with the mission statement up on the wall.

That sort of activity is a start, and usually done in good faith, but that's all it is — a good start. The real juice of a values-based organization, as I've said before, is in the dialogue. To be truly a values-based public service, we have to be living, breathing and working in a constant state of values-based management, values-based processes, values-based rewards, values-based behaviour and values-based results.

Values are not merely nice words that we throw in to add veracity to our reports. In public service, values are what we do.

In concluding this letter, I urge you to investigate, without delay, the real values of your organization. If you are a soldier, ask for more than just the current rules of engagement. Ask what we do when we find ourselves

Bureaucratically incorrect

Bureaucratically Incorrect

in a situation that has not been seen before. If you are a nurse, find out what values drive your health district, and if you work for the immigration department, explore what underlying values drive the everyday decision-making.

Finally, make a point of returning to your professional community periodically, as well. If you are a lawyer, teacher, accountant or surgeon, select your current reading as much for what is has to say about values as for what it says about techniques.

15 • Another Story

I'VE SAID BEFORE HOW MUCH I LOVE TO DISCOVER the secret lives of public servants. Chris Taylor was another one whose "other side" had great character.

Can a public servant have soul? Can a senior manager rock? Was Brian Wilson of the Beach Boys the greatest/writer producer of the 20th century? This is a little story about a senior manager with Health Canada who brought his soul to work every day. When Chris left us all too fast one summer, he left instructions insisting that those in attendance at his funeral take something home with them. He gave each person a copy of one of the greatest Beach Boy albums of all time. It was a take-home funeral souvenir.

"We all know that the foundation of our soul is built on love," Chris Taylor wrote in the eulogy that he left for his own funeral. It got to me that he'd written this himself. "Eulogies are not the easiest things to deliver, much less write," his words continued. No kidding, Chris!

Still, I was not surprised at this. I feel so privileged to have known and worked with Chris. He was my idea of a really great public servant. He was not one of the grey people. He worked in colour. He wanted to know what you had to offer and how it could work on his team. When we got together, he loved to talk policy, then have a little chat about organizational change and then got into the good stuff about Phil Specter's wall of sound.

If you knew Chris or worked with him, you knew he was a collector. He owned more than 15,000 vinyl albums. Chris prowled old record stores in every town he visited. He had a passion for the singers, the songs and how the music was produced. But what he really collected, I think, was colleagues and friends.

We know that people with passions are learners. People who are learners are usually also great teachers.

I learned much in a short time with Chris, and considered him both a colleague and a friend. Now I wish I could have spent more time with him. Lately, thinking of Chris has helped me remember the first occasion on which I realized public servants can have secret lives.

I was young and a public servant in Dauphin, Manitoba. My own similarly young family wanted a place in the country. Go see old Bill in the downtown office, suggested a co-worker. Bill was a quiet, somewhat timid accounting clerk who bothered no one, did his job and left no skid marks.

Sure, come out and see the place, he invited. We got there. Bill lived alone with his wife. She was heating up some dog food on the stove as we got there. Birds were flying around the room. The windows were nailed shut. I could imagine no worse life of desperation. I felt that I had stepped into a Kafka novel.

Towards the end of the evening, Bill invited me into his back room. "I want to show you something," he said, and pulled an old shoebox from under the bed. Please read, he insisted, and I began to pull out the most wonderful poems from that box. I sat in the presence of soul, of spirit dutifully put away each morning as he prepared for work, and returned to each evening under the light of the back room lamp.

I remember wondering why we couldn't have the poet in Bill inhabit the office, as well.

To me, Chris Taylor was the poet who came to work. He was only fifty-four years old. He was buried with a copy of the Beach Boys classic "Pet Sounds" album, and he went out as a teacher. He taught us that you can bring your soul into the workplace, you can manage people with spirit and discipline, and you can die well if you so choose.

When I talk about how we will recruit young people into the public service, I often bring up the legacy of Chris Taylor.

16 • Busyness

IT WAS ABOUT A DECADE AGO, AS I REMEMBER, that I first started using the modified Workout tool in our busy office. You may recall or know that the Workout is basically a systems tool designed to be a fast, focused and effective problem-solving practice. You get the right people — those holding knowledge on the subject — in the room, focus on one agenda item, and use skilled facilitation and work under pressure of time to a specified deadline. The next day, you take the recommendations produced to the decision-makers for a yes, a no, or needs-more-work response.

I found that once people had worked with it, they really started to like the technique. We were using it to successfully clear up issues that had festered in meetings and committees for months, even years.

What I remember most, however, was the response of one particular member of that staff. I'll call him Buzz. Buzz was the busiest guy in the office, or so it seemed. He was always flying down the hall, racing off to one meeting or another. His arms were always full of papers; his bulging briefcase kept his back in a permanent hunch.

He was the quintessential Mr. Busy. When I'd meet him in the hall, he would rush up, breathless and full of apology. "I am supposed to go to one of your workouts, Bob, but you know I am up to my ass in alligators these days," — his favourite expression du jour.

I would say no problem, feeling somewhat guilty for not being as busy or stressed out as him. This went on for quite a while — until I finally snapped.

Buzz again: "Sorry I can't make it to the session. My in-basket is just killing me." This time I looked him in the eye and told him he was a fool. He was shocked. I felt giddy. I was making a breakthrough. I asked him if he had been working late these days. "You bet," he said, "every night."

"Well," I repeated, "you are indeed a fool. You are working till nine o'clock every night driving a gas-guzzling, broken-down Hummer of a system. I am offering you a nimble, efficient and high-performing Japanese hybrid automobile."

He didn't get the metaphor.

"If you want to work late every night instead of taking one day to fix the system, then go ahead, but don't complain to me anymore about how busy you are."

Already in your short career, grasshopper, you have probably met a few of these characters. They are the busiest people on the floor. If you could actually work up a sweat in an office environment, they would be perspiring proudly.

Watch out for these people.

You must be careful not to confuse busyness with effectiveness. Busy people are not always the most effective. Effective people are not always the busiest.

I know some people are truly both; they are very busy and stunningly effective. But in my experience, the truly busy, effective people do not actually look that busy, overworked or stressed. They seem to have time for a conversation, a cup of coffee or a lunchtime stroll.

Interesting.

We have talked before about mental models. These are beliefs, assumptions or long-held ideas about how the world works. One of the all-time great mental models in organizations is the fallacy that busyness equals results. It is a powerful perspective. Many managers, brought up in an organizational culture that in many ways worshiped at the altar of busyness, have no other measuring stick for looking at staff effectiveness. If people appear busy, then all must be well; things must be getting done and progress must be being made. Well, be careful.

Another cautionary tale: I once worked for a manager who would have considered himself a results-based person. Sadly, however, he succeeded only in raising the level of stress, as opposed to team performance. As you can imagine, he and I were not really compatible. My greatest fault, in his view, was that I did not ever seem to be sufficiently busy or industrious. I was never at my desk, and shouldn't a busy public servant be at a desk, on task, on time and online?

So, he would show up looking for me and find an empty cubicle. "I believe I hear laughter down the hallway," pipes up the boss's favourite whom we called "The Snitch."

"He must be down there." And on it went.

The Snitch, being the favourite, was always on time. He came in early, booted up his computer, stayed busy until his allotted fifteen-minute break for coffee and half hour for lunch. Always there, always busy, he was this manager's delight. Even I was impressed.

But whatever I was doing must have had some validity because, within a year, I was given new responsibilities. In other words, however things looked on the surface, results were valued over face time.

I never thought twice about "The Snitch" till a few years later. I was on the phone with an old colleague and he asked me if I remembered "The Snitch." I did. He informed me that "The Snitch" had been let go. "Who did he kill?" I queried, mindful of the difficulties in letting people go.

"Oh, he didn't commit any homicide," my friend laughed, "but they found out he had been running a small business on that computer for years."

He was a busy guy alright.

Two of the biggest buzzwords these days are performance management and results-based approaches.

I spent many years in the field of education. You can run a classroom that looks good, where kids are well behaved, on task, quiet, at their desks and not shaking any boats. Whether they are learning anything or not is a different question altogether.

A good teacher is far more interested in what a child is learning than what a child is or is not doing.

In many of our organizations, we find some managers who run the office like a boarding school. As long as everyone is busy and looking good, we must be on track.

To get real results, grasshopper, you have to work smarter, not harder. The great American philosopher Mark Twain once wrote, "Thunder is good, thunder is impressive, but it is lightning that does the work."

The great Canadian philosopher Shania Twain says men spend too much energy trying to woo her, and "that don't impress me much." I have to agree with her. You have to do it right, not a lot. I am not impressed with the thunder and heavy breathing of the oh-so-busy person. I am way more interested in the lightning strikes of the quiet, effective ones.

These days, I often meet managers and front-line people who tell me they are working one hundred and ten per cent. That doesn't impress me much. How about working at a hundred per cent? Still leaves me cold.

I am looking for the person working at ninety per cent. Why?

Because that means they might be giving the remaining ten per cent to the critical job of fixing the organization's systems. If you are working flat out on operations at one hundred per cent, then who is fixing the system, fine-tuning the processes and coming up with creative, innovative ideas to get things done faster and better?

Sorry, gotta go now....busy, busy, busy.

17 • Words

REMEMBER WHEN CHUCK JONES DIED. At your age, you may or may not know who Chuck Jones was, but I'll give good odds that you know his work. Jones was one of the great animators of our generation. He gave us Bugs Bunny, Daffy Duck, the Roadrunner and many more, including my all time favourite, Pepe LePew.

When an interviewer once asked Jones if he considered himself an artist, Jones replied without equivocation, "No, I do not consider myself an artist." He then launched into a story about how the poet Robert Frost once chastised a young man who introduced himself as a poet, saying that the man could call himself a writer or scribbler, but the word poet was a "gift word." That is to say, you cannot bestow the word on yourself; it must be given by others.

Perhaps we all should take a deep breath and reflect on Frost's wisdom. Perhaps we should reexamine our great hurry to adopt new words for new organizations. Take, for example, some of the more popular words in the past decade: leader, mentor and even that ubiquitous word, team. If we were to check these against the perspective of Robert Frost's gift words, we might understand the frustration many of our colleagues feel at the disconnect between the words and reality.

When I wrote about leadership, I was careful to suggest that for someone to call himself a leader does not ring true. Try calling a "leadership meeting" instead of a "management meeting." Check the comfort level in the room. You can't mandate leadership. You cannot implement leadership. If someone says they are practicing leadership, you can almost see the smoke they are blowing. Much more realistic is to manage well, work hard, do the job, support one's people and take a risk. Do these things well, and there is a good chance you will be called a leader...as a gift from all of us. If you don't do your job well, sorry, but all the leadership seminars in the world won't help you.

The word team has a similar history. Imagine using the word "team" not to describe a business unit, but to describe those in the unit. You know those people down in internal audit? What a great team!

There are a lot of words we throw around without giving much thought to what they really mean. Perhaps the best way to get to use new words is through results, not a new program.

While you are at it, consider — as has the University of Minnesota — tossing out these words and phrases. I am sure you have your own word candidates — from the vocabulary in your workplace — for tossing as well.

I feel... the bottom line... learning resource centre... human resources... viable alternatives... at this point in time... input... sharing... perfectly candid... do-able... interface... task as a verb (I am tasking them)... outsourcing... revenue enhancement... conceptualize... user friendly... quality time... off-loading... debrief... functionality... oversight... outplacement... re-engineering... push the envelope... cyber... reinvent... closure... gaming... give one hundred and ten per cent... wake-up call... negative growth... health-care delivery... wellness... de-install... disenfranchise and ramp up.

There is a wonderful movement afoot — across the nation — to implement plain language, especially in public service. I found this award-winning example.

"[Name] informed you of the procedures for calculating interest for insufficient estimates. If the enclosed invoice(s) include charges for insufficient estimates, a detailed insufficient estimate used to calculate these charges is also enclosed."

Changed to:

"How to pay your bill: To avoid penalties as well as further interest, you must pay this bill by its due date."

And finally, on the numbers of words we think we need...a little note from an American correspondent...

- Pythagorean Theorem: .... 24 words
- Lord's Prayer: .... 66 words
- Archimedes' Principle: .... 67 words
- Ten Commandments: .... 179 words
- Gettysburg address: .... 286 words
- Declaration of Independence: .... 1,300 words
- US Government regulations on the sale of cabbage: . 26,911 words

In the age of the knowledge-based economy, words *are* our hard currency. Let us not just spend the loonies!

18 • Space

BACK IN 1992, I WAS FORTUNATE TO HAVE THE OPPORTUNITY to interview Peter Senge, and one of the questions I asked him was whether or not he felt he captured everything he wanted when he finished his monumental work, *The Fifth Discipline*.

Not at all, he said. "I wish I would have added a sixth discipline. A lot of work still needs to be done on what I call the learning vessel — the space where we work and learn."

I am beginning to have a better idea of what he meant by that, especially in these times of office-building downsizing, cubicle explosion and the cult of non-offensiveness.

Let's start by going back a few years. Public service buildings have been an affront to the aesthetic in all of us for years — first to those of us who must work in them every day, and second to those who need to visit them to get their business done.

Years ago, the designs for most government buildings, I swear, must have originated with the same government architects who designed prisons and mental hospitals. Bland brick structures with cement block corridors painted institutional beige. They were filled with wooden and metal furniture, designed (it seemed) to prevent injury or suicide attempts from the terminally bored. All this, of course, was topped off with the ubiquitous photo of Her Majesty in every boardroom. Needless to say, these buildings did not scream "innovation happening here every day."

Over the years, we have perked things up a bit, but we still have a phobic dread of colour, and art is just one of the guys down in finance. We continue to bathe in the continuous glow of hundreds of fluorescent lights. Every breath of air has been previously breathed by fellow workers; fresh air having no opportunity to reach workers through something as novel as a window that opens!

Perhaps you and your friends are in buildings of an altogether better design, that look and feel great, where light, colour, air, and space have been thought out, and make coming to work as fresh an experience as coming into the space where you live. (Well, where some of you live.) For most of us however, the workspace in which we spend our day can be somewhat less than interesting.

Let me be clear about something here. I do not advocate that every public-service office building be torn down and replaced with an architectural daydream.

Let's just try to keep up.

I must have experienced at least a dozen or more renovations in my thirty years of paradise. For the life of me, I don't believe that for at least ten of those renovation efforts, they did anything more than slap on a new coat of paint, put in new carpet and, if we were lucky, upgrade the cubicles to match the new colour scheme. Somehow, design was considered a frill and never seriously factored in to any budget.

Still, don't these people read the same magazines that you and I read? Once in a while, don't they even watch the designer guys on television, for Pete's sake? Creating a space for working — and more importantly, for thinking — is not rocket science, but it does involve thinking differently. I think we need some work here in a bunch of distinct areas.

For fun, let's start with the cafeteria. I just relocated to a city where the government office has a large cafeteria. I was anxious to try it out. The name of this cafeteria, I kid you not, is "The Sivil Service Kafeteria." Perhaps it was someone's idea of being cute? To me it implies, "Beware: illiterate, disrespectful, white supremacists are about to feed you." The food is definitely cafeteria-style. A daily offering of over-fried, bland and sorry-looking offerings would be snuggling against one another under the heat lamp for warmth. It doesn't get any better after a taste-test.

Others, I notice, have upgraded their buildings to include a food court. Great — now we don't even have to travel to a local mall for our daily intake of vapid; it comes to us.

There is a great story about public-sector food. Think for a quick minute: Where do we have to go to for the worst reputation in food, served in a public-service institution? You got it...hospitals.

So, I recall a story on the radio a few years ago where a newly appointed CEO of a hospital in the Rockies decided to take his lunch in the hospital cafeteria. He was not forced to, under contract. I believe he was just curious. He emerged appalled. As boss, he recognized the choice of returning to his habit of taking lunch in a local establishment more appropriate to his status and taste, or making the world he was being paid to work in more likely to reflect his own leadership styles and taste.

So he hired a chef. Cost a lot more. It must have freaked out the finance people and the communications people, who foresaw angry citizens storming the gates. Pretty risky for a public servant, but what happened? Well, soon the whole staff was eating lunch in the cafeteria, then staying late for dinner. They even started bringing their wives and friends to the cafeteria for dinner. Before long, healthy citizens in the town with no relatives in the hospital were frantically calling for reservations in the hospital cafeteria. A public-service joint!

I was delighted to read the other day that Jamie Oliver, the *Naked Chef*, has decided to direct some of his attention towards school cafeterias. Hopefully the hairnet ladies' days are numbered.

Another location is the boardroom. Take a good look at your average boardroom. What does it say to you? When I look at most boardrooms, I find they clamour "meeting, meeting, and meeting." This is just fine, if you need to hold a formal business meeting. However, business meetings comprise less than half of any day's meetings. We have hard-working, problem-solving meetings, informal conversational meetings, high-stress personnel meetings, coaching sessions, learning sessions, workshops and informal social gatherings. Isn't it always so special to celebrate a milestone event with pizza and pop around a hectare of polished maple under the ever-present gaze of our Monarch?

We obviously need boardrooms, but really, does every meeting room have to be a boardroom? What about a learning room with walls designed especially to stick things up on, a room equipped with all the techno gadgets as well as comfortable chairs and carpet? What about a dedicated space furnished with comfortable chairs, soft light and real art on the walls — exclusively for conversation? Why do we have to meet with clients or coach a colleague in a stiff, formal boardroom?

Well over a decade ago, in Ottawa, the Department of Indian and Northern Affairs had an architect consult with native elders, after which the architect designed a "kumik" on one of the top floors. It was a circular room, panelled in wood with subdued lighting, which, upon entry, immediately felt calm and respectful. The visiting elders worked out of there, but when there was no visiting elder, staff and visitors loved this space as a sanctuary from the tyranny of the boardroom. Two other departments have since followed this lead.

I believe the physical spaces we create in which to work, create the space in our heads in which to think. We talk about relationship management, but ninety percent of our conversations with each other are conducted across hardwood. It may be our desk, a counter top or a board table.

I hesitate to even mention cubicles. Dilbert has this field covered. Frankly, I don't believe they are going to go away anytime soon, so I believe we must learn to live with them. The trick is to not let them control the space. There is a tendency to follow design-based consistency with cubicles, then slavishly maintain that design imperative. I recall a manager going through the roof one day when he discovered that, after all his work to get the new colour-coded system, some fool had brought a different-coloured set of in-baskets that clashed with the standard black chosen to coordinate with the overall decor. It created a perfect hell in that workplace for days.

A colour scheme for office cubicles does not always mean that we must take away human beings' basic desire for individuality. I have seen managers put diversity into the strategic plan, but send out memos on how many personal photos you can hang in your egg crate.

So far, this chapter has been about physical space, but grasshopper, you and I know that this is not the real problem. The real challenge is the psychic and emotional space that we create in our workplaces. Our attitudes, values, behaviour, protocols and voice all contribute to a more complete definition of space.

Bureaucratically Incorrect

- Do we create space for conversation or managed communication?
- Do we create space for conformity or diversity?
- Do we create space for production or reflection?
- Do we create space for managing or for leadership at all levels?
- Do we create space for mediocrity or do we create a space for beauty?
- Do we create a space for competency or do we create space for mastery?
- Does our space scream boredom or does it sing creativity.

I believe Senge had these things in mind when he talked of the "learning vessel." To create a space where learning is the focus, conversation is paramount, quality is expected and respect lives and breathes every day, would be a good start to building a workplace learning vessel.

Remember, just as the little pig discovered, the walls of cubicles are not made of brick! So, like the big bad wolf, huff and puff a little and blow them off.

19 • Diversity

I THINK I FIRST MET HOWARD IN 1952. I would have been about five years old and he would have been a young adult. The first thing I noticed about Howard was he was different. He had a hump on his back and he walked on crutches, swinging his paralyzed legs between the sticks. I thought he was cool. Then I got to know him and I found out he was really cool! In a time before motorized wheelchairs, Howard invented and built his own little hand-operated car. This got him out to the fields where he operated a tractor all day long with hand controls that he had also designed. In a time before diversity, integration and accessibility in schools and public buildings, Howard enrolled in a correspondence course and became an accomplished electronic technician. He was also the first person in our community to obtain a special driver's license permitting him to pilot a hot, new Olds Rocket 88 equipped with hand controls. Funniest guy I've ever known.

When my cousin Garry and I used to sleep over at the farm, Howard did standup comedy — from a sit down position often until two in the morning. Those late night laughs under the coal oil lamp have yet to be matched.

So what is the point of my telling you this story? It is that I miss him and I find myself always looking around in my life and workplaces for another Howard. To my mind, there should be all kinds of Howard's out there, and we should be recruiting them. After all, he was an inventive genius, a self-starter, an independent thinker, a hard worker and a pleasure to be around. As I see it, Howard would have made an excellent public servant but, as you can imagine grasshopper, in those days he might not have exactly been the first in line for the interview. Today, of course, we have diversity programs to ensure he would get that chance...right?

Well, we have the programs all right and we have come a long way since 1953, but some of us — including my daughter who got her first public service job finding job placements for exceptional students — believe we still have a way to go.

A while ago, on a flight from Montreal, I met and struck up a conversation with a public service executive. He was African American and I had a hunch he may have some interesting stories. I was right. I listened with fascination to his description of the work he was undertaking with his staff to engender a sense of pride in their work. He would load them on busses and drive them through Windsor and point out where public service money and public service people were making a difference in their community. I ran into him again recently and he told me about his mother. Here, in his words, is her story.

The year was 1967 and it was not an easy time for a woman in search of employment. Certainly, it was not an easy time for a woman who had not had to look for work for twenty-one years. When you consider the woman in question was 55 years old, of African descent, a single parent with four mouths to feed, it was unquestionably not an easy time.

In 1967, Windsor, Ontario, like many other Canadian communities, was struggling to understand the racial tensions and upheavals that were highlighted in the media on almost a daily basis. Windsor was also one more community coming to grips with the changing role of women in the workforce. It was a struggle to put the needs of *all* people into perspective when the hiring patterns, historically, had been predicated on "veterans preference" and "hiring the best man for the job." It was a community that still considered those over forty as "middle-aged" and not likely candidates for entry-level positions.

Into that labour market comes Alice Anna Allen. Alice was born on October 5, 1912 to an African-American man and his German wife. In 1954, her 37 year-old husband died suddenly, leaving her with four children, aged between 6 years and 10 months. Alice was not one to feel sorry for her self. Her mother had taught her to be strong and to "do what you have to do." Alice had to take care of her children, and she knew she had to do this herself. So, on the day after their father's death, despite her grief, Alice's children still enjoyed homemade birthday cake to mark their sister's 5th birthday. Though the family received social assistance benefits for thirteen years, and didn't have money for extras, Alice's children never knew they were poor. They had clean clothes and healthy food to eat, and a mother who cared for them. Alice never re-married, devoting all her attention and energy to raising children who would come to contribute in very meaningful ways to their father's memory and to their community. She taught them love, self-respect, and respect for others and instilled in them all both a sense of humor and a social conscience.

When her youngest child started high school, Alice determined to go back to work. It was 1967, and not an easy thing for a Black, single woman with no recent work history — one who was 55 years old. Alice didn't even think to say "I can't" or "they won't hire me." She met with the staff of the Windsor office of Revenue Canada Taxation. Fortunately for Alice, they didn't see an older, Black, single mother with no recent work history. They saw an individual who brought to her interview excellent test scores, a keen sense of duty and responsibility and a wonderful sense of humor. They saw someone who would not give up on a task that seemed a bit difficult on first inspection. They saw a person who could contribute to the organization's goals, and who could do it in an exemplary fashion.

The staff of the Windsor office of Revenue Canada Taxation recognized the need for what we now call "diversity" and embraced it with open arms. They didn't feel that they were taking a chance — they knew they had hit the jackpot with Alice Anna Allen. Today all four of Alice's children have completed their education and each of them is successfully contributing to their respective community in a professional position of employment.

It is a strange incomplete business, this diversity issue. It upsets me to have to say this, my friend, but the odds are still high that one day soon, over a cup of coffee, one of your colleagues may start in on you about how one has to be a different colour, gender or whatever to get a job or get ahead in this organization.

Hold your temper, take it easy! This could open up into a good conversation. Not a conversation, if you can help it, about bad manners, or some form of "ism" or even about compassion. This is a good time for a great conversation about business needs, hard bottom lines and artistry in organization.

Whoa! I sense I may have just lost you there. Artistry? What is that about?

Tomson Highway is a Cree playwright, raised on a trap line in Northern Manitoba, who lives part time in France, speaks French fluently and would be as comfortable in a Gay Pride March in downtown Toronto as in the Grand March of a pow wow in northern Manitoba.

He is diversity incarnate!

Recently, I heard him address a large crowd of public servants on the subject of diversity. He has a unique view on this issue and one that may be important for other Canadians to hear.

Tomson compared the violent and brutal history of monocultural European countries with our more recent and multicultural history. He spoke about the thousands of years of wars and hatred in the struggle against difference in Europe. We were reminded of the madness inherent in ruling families who have practiced purity of race, leading to a gene pool with no deep end, that fuelled the craziness and left so many of our ancestors with no choice but to flee to a New World...paradise.

Paradise, he says, where different people were welcomed and assimilated by those people who were already here. It was an unsullied place to create a new race of even more beautiful people, once they decide to mix it up a little. Thank goodness for cold winters.

Tomson Highway has no use — he told us — for ghettoized thinking. He warned us that intellectual, spiritual and social inbreeding still exists, including within the workplace. It is not uniformity that makes the world turn; it is difference that makes it work and makes it beautiful. Vive la différence! He sees the mixing of worldviews, spiritual, social and intellectual ideas as the mix that will help us build what he calls a Code of Honour that works for all human beings.

Finally, says Tomson Highway, there are certain people who help keep the fires alive. The shamans in First Nations culture, were neither hard edged men or women, nor strongly hunter or warrior. Shamans could not be easily categorized, but their role was respected as one who helped soften the edges of the community, hold a reflection back to others and show a new way of being. The shaman, the artist, was simply a different character albeit one whose difference was critical to the community.

Another friend of mine, himself the product of the attraction of difference is my aboriginal colleague Kelly Lendsay. Kelly practices leadership and organizational change in this country and is a leading innovator in building new ideas and relationships in the field of socioeconomics.

I watched him work, one morning, with a group of high-powered bankers, executives and other suits of assorted stripes. He was blunt. Don't be hiring First Nation people to help make you feel good or to hit the marks on your diversity goals, he challenged. Do it for your R.O.I. (Return on Inclusion.) Diversity pays, not costs. As an example, he used the experiences of Weyerhauser and Syncrude who found that their entry into global markets, the increase in creative thinking and the growth of a harmonious culture could only be achieved by becoming a fully diversified workforce.

Kelly talks about the inclusion/exclusion dynamic as the key to a new vision. For too long, exclusion was the experience of those who were different. We created cultures of exclusion that must now be replaced with a different culture of inclusion. It is not just about those with differing colour, language or beliefs. Kelly suggests asking a white middle aged male if he feels included in his workplace. Quite often he does not. If that were prevalent, then why would we subject a Cree woman, or an Ethiopian man, or a blind person to that same environment. We have to create and build this culture of inclusion as we start to fill it — so says Kelly.

Finally, my friend, diversity comes back to my favourite subject…learning. A recent conversation with my colleague Karen provoked her to recall a woman whose first language was not English. Karen related to me how she had to slow down, listen, and pay attention in order to work effectively with this woman. Well, no surprises there, we both realized. In order to work more successfully with everyone on our team, we all have to slow down, listen and pay close attention.

One of the most powerful means of learning is to be faced with difference. It makes us stronger, it sharpens our skills and it invites the possibility of finding solutions above and beyond the ordinary.

Bureaucratically Incorrect

In the ecosystem we know that diversity gives strength and leads to a greater chance of survival. Monocultures tend to get sick. Communities and workplaces are no different. Look at the multicultural cities that thrive like Vancouver and Toronto compared to towns and cities that lack diversity. In one generation, we find that children of new immigrants are fully "Canadianized." In ten years, the bulk of our workforce will rely heavily on immigration. I know that I have met far too many cab drivers with engineering degrees. What a waste of intellectual capital! Canadians are so far ahead of other countries with this stuff that we may actually suffer more from a problem of complacency. We lead, but we can do so much better. Surveys tell us that your generation is more colourblind, more tolerant and perhaps more open than any previous cohort. So, don't be afraid to crank it up a notch once you get the chance. I look forward to your generation doing things because it is the right thing to do not just because we have a program or policy to implement.

2o • Practice

LMOST A DECADE AGO, IN HIS BOOK, *Job Shift*, William Bridges suggested that "today's organization is rapidly being transformed from a structure built out of jobs to a field of work needing to be done." I am not sure we have yet grasped the fullness of this concept. People are still pretty tightly bound to their jobs, job description, classification and turf. In the meantime, the public service is changing around us. The industrial model of breaking work into pieces, assembly line style, left us incredibly vulnerable when downsizing and reorganization hit. The latter eliminated certain jobs while the former left a reduced workforce to complete the "work to be done." This whole concept represents a huge mental model that will take many years to fully change. Still, we recognize that we have to begin somewhere, and recent activity and renewal within Human Resources Management would indicate a sleeping giant beginning to stir.

Lately, I have been thinking about the concept of practice. Peter Senge used the word in reference to learning-organization theory as a critical element in learning theory. Musicians practice, sports teams practice, even pilots practice, but mangers with million-dollar budgets that are involved in critical areas of public policy — are not given much chance to practice. Most of our work is in real time. This can create a huge learning gap as you live with the results in real time. But there is another definition of practice that interests me even more. The word practice can also describe your life's work, your calling as opposed to your job. We used to speak of a doctor building a practice, or a negotiator building a practice.

In my own work life, and in that of my colleagues, I have noticed there are often two streams to our work. The job stream is self-evident. It is defined through job descriptions, classification, our manager's immediate needs and the incessant constraints of the in-basket and e-mail. Despite all of this, we may find that little seeds have sprouted in the fetid soil where some of our colleagues are concerned. Someone in a policy shop develops a passion for large-group facilitation. Another in finance becomes fascinated with dispute resolution, or a manger in Human Resources becomes intrigued with the application of technology.

They now have a choice. They can grow their passion and their thirst for a greater knowledge and facility in their area of interest that may have nothing to do with what's outlined in their job description. Often this is all done on their own time or they can sneak in some learning during downtimes in the office. Should they opt for learning during the "downtimes," eventually, they are likely to encounter one of two types of reactions. The first goes along the lines of, "That stuff is not connected to your real job, and if I find you doing that sort of thing, it must mean you do not have enough real work to do." Or, they may be praised for their initiative: "This is great. How can we help you learn more and start to gain some real advantages from your new skills and knowledge?"

It is obvious which reaction conforms to a learning organization. It is also painfully true that for many employees, the first reaction is the norm. Consider a young manager with whom I spoke recently. He had been invited to speak at a convention on youth initiatives in public service. He is a young, successful manager and was offered the out-of-province trip on an all-expenses paid basis. As you might imagine, he was shocked when his supervisor flatly refused to let him go, saying she needed him for crisis work in the office these days and his work was here, not there. His appeals went nowhere. He ended up staying in the office. There was no crisis, everyone else was there as well. That young person is now with another department, and I am sure the old department wonders why he is gone or maybe not.

For every story like this, there are others about managers who not only encourage their staff to work outside their cubicles, but who actively promote a more corporate approach to staff deployment.

I would like to think of these external, peripheral learning passions as our individual practice. I do not believe they have to conflict with our jobs;

in many ways, they will enhance our jobs and provide the sanity and motivation to keep us sharp.

My practice was building learning organizations. My real job was in Executive Services. My practice started out small. A Workout here, an OpenSpace there. My manager, Sandy Thomson, would encourage me to keep working on the practice stuff. Soon the credibility of the practice started to reflect back on our team and the department. Later, this was judged by others — all the way up to the top — as a good thing. It still is and I have been fully supported in my practice by my Department.

For some, the practice will always remain a small part of work life. For others, it may take over and become their work life. Those for whom their real work is their practice are truly blessed. There are thousands of public servants out there who have either thought about developing an individual practice (perhaps not using the word) or have begun to build one. Sometimes, the practice is close to their real job, like the accountant who is fascinated with forensic accounting as well as all the other aspects of accounting which comprise her formal job description. Conversely, an employee's job and practice can also be quite disparate, as with the file clerk who is taking a night course in mediation.

We are going to have to come to grips with this phenomenon of practice. Those who remain stuck in the traditional organization, see an individual practice as a threat to the work at hand, the team and the department. Let's begin to see it from a learning-organization perspective. Let us start to see it as an enhancement to our work, credibility, team depth and, most importantly, a real corporate contribution to the public service at large.

This then is the concept of individual practice. Our job is our work and our practice is our passion.

Sometimes, organizations have been a little slow to understand and appreciate the added value of bringing ones practice more to the foreground in our place of work. Not so today.

The pressure is on to manage knowledge and to create a continuous learning culture that will give us the edge in managing that knowledge.

Sometimes the simplest ideas are the strongest and so it is with the emerging concept of communities of practice. One of the leading thinkers

Bureaucratically Incorrect

in this area, Etienne Wenger, tells us right off the mark that this idea is not really so new. For centuries, we have had guilds and associations and other more formal models of organization for people with a common practice. Still do.

One of the difficulties with the older models was time. Joining an association sometimes felt like an added burden...one more thing on an already full plate. Today's communities of practice try to avoid that structural handicap and have adopted a more informal approach with an emphasis on growing relationships and knowledge sharing rather than commitment to an organization.

However, the "what's in it for me," mindset is also most apparent as people hesitate to join anything these days that piles on yet another obligation. What we may not have realized is the "what's in it for me" got people connected and committed but the real benefits were to the whole organization as the community connections started to move the knowledge across the organization as well as up and down.

Think for a minute about where we would find communities of practice.

I like to see them in a geographic context. For example there may be sixty-seven forensic accountants in Halifax. Perhaps twenty three in the federal government, twenty in the provincial government, four in municipal and the rest in the private sector. How many of these forensic accountants know one another even if they live in the same community? What sort of professional learning, best practice exchange and idea generation would happen if we could get just one third of them together over breakfast just once a month?

How many strategic planners are there in Ottawa? How many know one another? How many language instructors in Montreal? How many budget analysts in Winnipeg? Hey, how many meeting planners in your own organization? Are they talking? Do they know one another? Where do they get their information?

One of the fundamental principles of learning organizations is that your best knowledge is in-house and often involved in front line service delivery. This is easy to say but hard to put into practice.

Communities of practice represent a simple, cost effective, learning-centred tool to investigate areas of concern. So, what are some fundamental principles around organizing communities of practice? Well, for a start...

* Membership is voluntary.
* Structure is informal.
* Leadership is critical but must be organic and community-centred.
* Executive and corporate support is crucial.
* Communities of practice promote knowledge sharing both horizontally as well as vertically.
* communities of practice learn differently and more importantly, they become strategic in their learning thus benefiting members as workers/employees but also contributing to the strategic goals of the organization.
* Communities of practice attract even more practitioners and the community now starts to provide the juice to attract talent, build loyalty and retain people in the practice.
* A community of practice has a domain that is its shared area of concern or work.

Today there are hundreds of "communities of practice" growing across the Canadian public service. For me the light turned on when I recognized the need to find and train new learning organization practitioners. I struggled with the old "train the trainer" model and found it cumbersome and loaded with the baggage of old style learning methodologies.

My colleague, Karen Bonner, introduced me to the community of practice model and we began to experiment. Today there are over one hundred practitioners located in every province. The organization, the commitment and the learning is completely in their hands as a community. The results are amazing. People do not want to learn in a vacuum. Workshops can be such a vacuum. They really start to learn when they find a passion for a subject and then make a real connection with other learners and real time practitioners. The community of practice gives them both...in spades. So grasshopper, all you will need to know right now is...

Bureaucratically incorrect

- What is my practice?
- Who else does it?
- How can I get them into a room?
- Where can I/we get a little leadership and coaching to help me/us grow this thing?

After that, you will be introduced to the emerging world of communities of practice online and you will never look back.

And finally, here is the really good news. It is cost effective. The community of practice on coaching is off and running across Canada and there's not been a dent in anyone's budget. The really, really good news is that if some of us can help it, this will never become a government program. Why? Well first of all we only have so much money to spend on improvement programs and we can avoid cutting into those funds. More important still, to those of us in the underground working to build these communities, is our fervent desire to keep them away from the program model and try to make them a normal part of the workplace culture. The juice comes from the participants and the support comes from the leadership.

21 • Time

URING CONVERSATIONS WITH COLLEAGUES, over the years, I have found that the number one disease — affecting people in the workplace — is the waste, misuse and disrespect of people's time.

Time is a problem affecting us both negatively and positively. If we don't have enough time, it causes stress, and if we have too much time on our hands, it also causes stress. (As in, "If I am not busy enough, then how long will it be until they cut this job out of the action?")

So, we have to find a way to wrestle this time thing to the ground. Face it; it has been tried before. Heaven knows there are more courses out there than you can shake a stick at on time management. And of course you can go out and buy the latest iteration of Palm Pilot or Blackberry or some other device for personal organization.

Will these toys solve your time dilemma? Don't hold your breath! I am not convinced they will. First of all, the workshops and the baby computers are designed to organize your time. That's it. That's all.

They will organize your day, buzz you and slot you in. This is helpful, a little. But they will not manage your time. Let me put it like this. Today, you have scheduled six meetings, a visit to the research library, plus numerous other activities. Time organization will help you slot these into your cramped day. And that may or may not work out fine for you.

Real time management is more concerned with the nature, priority and actual need for those activities, than in how they fit into your day.

Let me give you an alternate scenario. First of all, let's assume that you connect with your team in the morning Standup. The Standup should also have given you some sense of team tasks and priorities, for the week perhaps, but certainly for the next eight hours. The standup should also have given you valuable intelligence about your own day as well. You took a few minutes and revisited all of your scheduled meetings and appointments. You then ranked them in order of priority. You realized that one of the six meetings was of relatively low priority, and that it could be postponed or possibly cancelled. Two of the remaining five meetings really weren't required at all. They should have been problem-solving sessions in need of re-design as action and time-based workouts. A further meeting could be re-jigged as a quick hallway standup. The briefing scheduled for three o'clock could be better accomplished and accomplished faster as a twelve-minute briefing.

The remaining two meetings were critical. You determined that for one of them, you could and should make a little more time available. As for the research visit, it could now be set aside by the revised schedule of meetings — which now offered greater flexibility.

You see, the problem here is fundamentally a tool problem. I have been saying this for years, and you must be tired of hearing it, but the three tools that are killing us in the workplace are meetings, committees and workshops. Meeting fatigue has everyone on edge. Committees seem to go on and on, and it's not uncommon for members to spend more time trying to figure out when they are all available to meet again, than meeting again. Workshops, as I have discussed in a previous chapter, are great time-wasters if they are focused less on the real business needs of the participants than they are on the content/design of the workshop presenter.

Back to time management, then. If you agree with me that all a fast, electronic organizer does is organize the "crap" a little better and faster, then we have work to do!

So, grasshopper, we must begin to challenge not only the content of our work, but the basic processes of our work as well. If you "get" this, in many ways, it pays for the rest of the book.

Remember how I earlier mentioned that public servants are knowledge workers? Well, here is where the rubber hits the road. Most of what we do in a day centres on managing, locating, collecting, editing, distributing, ingesting and creating new knowledge!

We do that with other human beings, for the most part. And we generally do it — as I've said before — with bad tools.

- Briefing notes are not brief.
- Meetings are undisciplined, unfocused and sometimes even inappropriate.
- Committees lack mandate, decision capacity and endpoints.
- Processes are full of red tape, bottlenecks and duplication.
- Decision-making has no consistent protocols.
- Dispute resolution has no agreed-upon protocol, structure or skilled personnel.
- Service standards are lacking at both the personal and team level.

These are but a few areas where real time gets wasted. No Palm Pilot in the world can help you here. You are going to need a full belt of modern power tools such as workouts, process mapping, charters, Standups, large group facilitation and twelve-minute briefings and interviews.

Before we can really deal with time management, we have to understand that our problems with time exist primarily with our workplace structure. Change these structures, and we will begin to pin the time opponent to the mat.

We also have to deal with mental models about time. Over the years, mental models like "bigger is better" have given us the wonderful three-pound research proposal, the lovely three-hundred-page policy document and the ever-popular thirteen-page job description!

Go back with me, once again, to the knowledge management model. Knowledge management consists of taking masses of data and sorting it out into large but more manageable chunks of information. More refined knowledge management finds a way to take these large chunks of information and turns them into smaller, usable chunks of knowledge. Then real knowledge management uses the intelligence of the organization, its partners and clients, and reduces these much smaller chunks of knowledge into gems of wisdom.

This is really hard work and, without question, it's a process that requires new tools and structures. I believe the learning organization is the cornerstone model for building a public service that does a good job. It must also remain a service that is consistently recreating its own structure and processes so that the service itself evolves and continues to improve. The payoff is that the organization becomes more knowledgeable and sophisticated in the process. Just one last thought on the flip side of time management. Remember the person with too much time on their hands — the one who becomes stressed out! Just the other day a former colleague and I reconnected and we began reminiscing about a department where we had both worked. Among the departmental personnel who shared our office were a group of specialists in economic development, a very highly paid category at the time.

However, the times, as it were, had put economic development somewhat off the organizational map. No initiatives, no programs, no money! These folks did not have a lot to do. Hard to believe, but it happens.

It wasn't their fault, necessarily, but they were resented by others for their modest workload. Some took advantage of the lull with extra long coffee breaks, and others were frustrated and spent hours on their networks and resume writing. Nothing changed for them for quite a long time. They were all victims of the job-description or program-description driven workplace.

Today, savvy, knowledge-based management, coupled with a work-focus instead of a job-description focus would mobilize this group. Their natural intelligence and the gift of extra time would lead them to search for work in support of other initiatives. They would, perhaps, talk to their clients and help them find new, helpful strategies. They may create some idea teams to look at innovation, or help start a new research project. Sitting and waiting for the world to change or for a new job description should no longer be an option.

Time, my friend, I say again, is our most precious commodity on the floor of the public service workplace. We ignore it at our peril. We also continue, at our peril, to plough through late nights and take work home on the weekend instead of mastering new tools that would enable us to work more efficiently.

22 • Rights

OVER THE YEARS, PUBLIC SERVANTS HAVE FOUGHT FOR — and won — some impressive victories to establish a solid foundation for workers' rights and fair labour practices in the public-sector workplace. It has not always been so, but today, our labour management relations and benefits are as good as any in the private sector — maybe better.

We have the right to organize, to advocate and to withdraw our services in the pursuit of an equitable agreement, with some exceptions around public safety and essential services. Inside these agreements are generous provisions for holidays, various leave programs, allowance provisions and reimbursements. Do not take them lightly. They were not obtained without struggle. Cherish them and do not take them for granted. The woman I love has worked professionally in a small business for about twenty years. After all this time, she only gets two weeks holiday with pay — and this thanks to government regulations, not employer largesse — no sick leave and, if she should fall ill with the flu, not only is she miserable, but she will pay for it later on her paycheque!

As a public servant, you have some of the most robust internal human resources policies in existence, covering such issues as overtime, harassment protection, parental leave and gender equity. You have an HR infrastructure that supports pension plans that won't be Enron'd! People move quickly to resolve any health and safety issues. Buildings have been torn apart to get at toxic mould in the walls which were making the occupants sick.

Compensation is always a conversation starter. Let's face it you have a right to a competitive salary. You may feel underpaid, but you might want to check out the difference, let's say, between the salary of a social worker in the public service and a social worker in the not-for-profit sector, or one working in a care home in the private sector. Generally speaking, we do quite well on all the important fronts. Indeed, some people think we may have it a bit too good. The critics argue that public service has become a little fat and lazy and suggest we may have, inadvertently, created a culture of entitlement in our workplace. This culture of entitlement may be leading, they surmise, to a workplace culture that supports a vigorous environment for grievances and redress overlaid with a litany of self-perceived employee-rights violations. This is often quite real not simply imagined. I know we are on thin ice here, grasshopper, but you might as well hear about this "victim mentality" from me as anyone else. Otherwise, you are liable to hear it in the halls and cubicles and in the very fabric of your new workplace — which would be worse. Every workplace is different and God bless you if yours is not tainted with the slightly acrid odours of incipient victim hood. You are fortunate indeed!

If not, well, right about now you are probably making internal choices about how you will respond to the slings and arrows in your employee–employer relationship. Let's try and approach this in a measured way — with balance.

In his book, *Man's Search for Meaning*, Victor Frankel wrote some of the most important words written to-date on the human response to evil. Essentially, he saw that survival was tied to one's image of oneself as a victim or victor. In his later years he was so bold as to suggest that America would do well to balance the Statue of Liberty on one coast with a Statue of Responsibility on the other. I am sure he recognized, from hard-won experience, that freedom requires as much work and accountability from those living in freedom as it requires from those governing the free. Rights are not a one-way street. They never have been. Without an equal dose of responsibility, the granting of new rights tends to fall on rocky soil. The shift to rights without a shift as well in responsibility can lead to a culture of entitlement without obligation. We must be vigilant in the public sector to maintain a continual conversation around this balance in our workplace.

Before I get off on my responsibility rant, let me assure you understand that I fully acknowledge we still have problems in the workplace.

Harassment, unfairness, poor treatment, overwork and inadequate compensation all still exist! Diligence continues to be required.

I remember a fabulous Deputy Minister who introduced me to many ideas about leadership. Peter Harrison was always being invited to speak at events and functions. I recall a particularly interesting request was presented to him. The event happened to be scheduled on a Sunday. Peter asked his assistant to send an acknowledgement, politely declining the invitation, and stating his reason: that family time and commitments had always taken precedence on Sundays. Afterwards, and still curious, Peter did a little more information gathering on the event. He discovered that the conference was one focusing on work/life balance, and more than three-quarters of the delegates were women. The real kicker was the conference took place on Mother's Day! So you ask a large number of mothers to leave home for a weekend that is in conflict with the one special day of the year set aside for their recognition, as mothers, by their respective families!

Stupidity abounds in our organizations. Thoughtlessness, inflexibility and just plain meanness can add to an already tough workday. Nevertheless, we already have many good programs and policies to tackle these things. I'd like to contribute a few bricks to that West Coast Statue of Responsibility, and do so from a public service perspective. If we had a few decades to build up the ideal list of public service responsibilities, what would we add to the list? Well, I can think of a few things.

Refer back to the chapter on public service ethics for a minute. Are these ethics just well meaning, high-sounding words packaged nicely by insightful leaders like the late John Tait? Do they mean we should hold more workshops, throw more instructions about ethics out there and hope that they stick? Of course not! You and I have to know these ethics, work these ethics, live and breathe these ethics. Ethics are not a series of workshops; they are a deep personal responsibility, and we should, on a daily basis, be held accountable for our ethical practice to the same extent as we hold our supervisors accountable for defending/upholding our rights.

Change management is another area of personal responsibility. No longer can change be expected from, attributed to and whined about as having come down to us from on high. Change affects us all, and we all have to do our part to manage it effectively.

I am getting so very tired of running forums on change that people don't attend because attendance is optional. We've become overly sensitive about individual rights; so much so that we don't force people to attend. But how the heck can that work?

When we run a session likely to have a major effect on how we do business, change the culture or plan our future, don't all of us have a responsibility to be in attendance? Shouldn't our leaders expect this as part of our work? Typically, I've noticed that a third or more of employees stay in the office when such forums are scheduled. They are either not interested, they're in love with their in-baskets, or they have a plain old "screw it" attitude. Yet these same people are among some of the first individuals to scream about their rights if the change/s made as a result of the meeting they elected to miss do not make sense or displease them?

Imagine a society where every citizen actually exercised his or her right to vote? Did you know that Jean Chrétien was elected with 24% of the eligible vote. Ralph Klein was elected with around 30%, and Dave Bronconnier, the mayor of Calgary, was elected with just 9% of the eligible vote. Where are the rest of the citizens on voting day and how would our public service and government look if all those eligible to vote actually exercised their democratic responsibility. Voting could be seen as just one of many bricks in that imaginary Statue of Responsibility — a statue that is fading in our civil society — and in our civil public service. You cannot manage change from the bleachers. It is not a spectator sport. Everyone has to play. You have to be willing to get your hands dirty. Everyone has a responsibility to think.

When I was a kid, (whoops, I was not going to say that), one of the first jobs available was that of a farmhand. Note the "hand" part of the word; the employer didn't want my head, just my hands! One day my brother tried to tell my uncle — a somewhat stubborn old farmer — that it was unsafe to pound a picket with your bare hands when using another poisoned bluestone picket as the hammer! He got a stoic look along with the admonishment, "You are not paid to think, my boy; I will do the thinking and you do the pounding." Six hours later, my brother was rushed to the hospital with a fast-moving red streak of blood poisoning racing toward his heart. My brother survived and learned something, not so, alas, my uncle.

In a traditional organization, those at the top were paid to think; those at the bottom were paid to do. Today's learning organizations require everyone to think. Believe it or not, there are still people in our workplaces who do not want to do this. Thinking, they feel, is not in their job description. Oh, wait a minute, now that I think about it, it actually isn't in their job description. Interesting!

Anyway, grasshopper, you have to change all this.

Above all, you must take responsibility for the application of common sense. Don't wring your hands at bad managers. Speak up. Don't bellyache at coffee about ineffectiveness or red tape; speak up or organize a workout. Don't accept substandard work. Pull the team together and boost the service standards in your team charter.

Don't moan about a lack of communication; take responsibility and get people talking. You know the tools by now. And for goodness sake, leave your baggage at home. The public sector workplace is there to serve citizens. No more and no less! Strive to provide better and better service every year and do not expect the workplace to help you straighten out your kid, organize your husband or make you feel better about getting old.

Do good work, take responsibility to improve that work, and hold onto your rights.

23 • Mentors

YOU MAY RECALL THAT IN A PREVIOUS LETTER ON WORDS, I recounted the story of Robert Frost and his wonderful notion of the "gift word." These are words that are preferably earned as opposed to assumed.

I find that "mentor" is another such word.

The other day, in my head office, I saw a poster advertising the organization's mentorship program. Frankly, it left me a little cold. For some reason, I have a hard time imagining "mentoring" as a government program.

But isn't that always the way in large public-sector organizations? Along comes a great idea or even just a hot word, and our immediate response is to turn it into a program or a training course. We have done it with teams, leadership, innovation and countless other valuable concepts.

Mentoring is one worth fighting back on, I believe.

Let me explain my thinking on this.

Excluding family and close friends, I have had just two mentors in my life. The first was a character I met in my first public-service job, teaching "sweat hogs" (a la Welcome Back Kotter) in Churchill, Manitoba in 1969. His name was Les Osland, and he was an orderly in the local hospital. I recall he had six kids. (The oldest, Gord, has been one of Canada's premiere rock and roll drummers for years.)

Les used to say he had lots of kids because he was the only CCF (the grandfather party of the New Democrats) guy in the Navy, so they kept him at sea more than necessary to keep him from stirring up trouble. Shore-leave time was precious, and babies were an inevitable, natural consequence.

He was big-boned, with wide grin, a shock of graying hair and charisma wafting from every pore. He was afraid of nothing, and I thought he was wonderful. His best friend was a Cree named Jack Robinson — another man of considerable physical stature — who introduced me to the wonderful world of First Nations humor and earthy philosophy. Both these men were characters, and I knew if I hung out with them, I would learn something important.

So I did — hang out with them!

Les had no formal education, but that didn't faze him a bit. He loved to read the career section of the classifieds and imagine which job would take him out of the bedpan-emptying business. One day, on coffee row, he announced that he had applied for the top position in the local Indian Affairs regional office. We indulged him his fantasy, but recognized the impossibility.

A month later, he got the job.

Let me try and explain how this happened. A group of Dene had been — ultimately tragically — relocated from their traditional lands into the town of Churchill. The result: incidences of alcoholism and violence spiked markedly. When the interview board asked Les what he would do about this, he told them he'd lead them back to the land from whence they had come.

Indian Affairs hired him. He did what he said he would do, and those people are doing much better today in their ancestral homelands in northern Manitoba. Les moved on to serve as an MLA in the Schreyer NDP government, but eventually got into trouble for being the contrarian he always was, even in a social democratic government!

On retirement, Les and his wife Doreen took a well-deserved break from politics, managing a home for mentally handicapped adults. He died some years ago but he walks with me every day.

Bill Alexander was the man who introduced me to the concept of continuous learning, and the power of conversation and dialogue. Bill was one of my professors at the University of Toronto OISE, and he was a classic! An immigrant academic mensch from Chicago, he spent his whole life learning his way into and out of the world of big ideas. Rumpled, bright and loving, he could listen you to a standstill. He was a great teacher because he was an even greater listener and learner. Bill was not about teaching us, but about getting us involved with and excited over what he was learning.

A number of years ago, after he had been diagnosed with prostate cancer, he went on something of a learning rampage and beat it. Along with another couple of companions, Hugh and Heather, I remember celebrating his victory in an ice-fishing hut on a big, frozen lake outside Toronto. It was an amazing moment.

Bill and Heather were sort-of Buddhists. Hugh and I were sort-of fishermen. The issue of worms became quite metaphysical as the would-be Buddhists pondered the existential implications of the worm on the hook, and we fishermen pondered the existential implications of either of the Buddhists actually catching a live, wriggling fish on the wormed hook.

It was a fine time.

A year later, Bill's doctors delivered good news — the prostate cancer remained in remission — and bad news: he now had lung cancer. It didn't look hopeful. So Bill went on another learning firestorm. During one visit, I recall hearing him call upstairs to his son to help him find that Lyle Lovett tape with the song that kicks off, "I haven't seen so many people in one place since the last time somebody died." He insisted he was going to have it played at his funeral. Then he suggested we head out for a visit to the Mt. Pleasant cemetery to check out his plot. It felt pretty nuts to sit down on the grassy earth with Bill, and wonder about the inhabitants in the adjacent plots.

Then it hit me...This guy is still teaching me, teaching me how to die. Later on, when he was close to the end, I was fortunate enough to be granted one last visit. I felt sober, sad and unsure of what to say. I decided to thank him for insisting that, now I was of a certain age, I too should go for the old "film noir," or colonoscopy, as it is properly known.

He wasn't supposed to talk, but he had to. He pulled me close and whispered that old joke about the two-finger rectal exam, with the punch line about getting a second opinion.

Just couldn't stop teaching.

Les and Bill. Two mentors. I'd never have found these guys in a mentoring workshop or program...not in a million years.

It seems to me that mentors are the end result of a truly fine teaching and learning relationship. Heaven knows, good relationships require attraction, time and hard work. You cannot decide to become a mentor. You live your life, you teach, you model behaviour and when you connect, when you touch someone, when you invest in the relationship...down the road they may feel about you as I feel about Les and Bill. You will become a mentor not by signing up, but by stepping up and building a relationship with someone you like, respect and want to learn from.

Grasshopper, find a mentor the natural way. First, be prepared to see people as they really are, not as they look and not according to whether they occupy important space. Look for character. Look for learners. Look for passion and compassion.

Get to know them. Ask for nothing. Offer lots.

And find dead mentors, too — in books, of course.

Find a mentor younger than yourself. Years ago, I found a young fisherman casting his fly line into Doctor's Pool in North Vancouver. Because I asked, he taught me more about fly fishing in an hour than I had learned in the previous six months.

And finally, be a mentor. Yes, you.

You have talent, you are a learner and you have passion. Someone needs you.

Watch for them.

Conclusion

SO, THERE IT IS.

You may have liked or hated it, but I hope you read it and didn't just skip to the end like it was a mystery novel!

I also trust it has provoked your thinking about public service and your decision to become a public servant. As I was writing the final chapters, the contracting scandals were picking up speed. Innovation, fresh thinking and new ways of doing business are once again, in danger of being seen as the enemy of the a renewed focus on accountability. It will be a shame if they are not both seen as important bookends to the whole collection.

There are, of course, no right or wrong answers or ideas in the book, only the views of one aging public servant. I'd like to think, however, that my thoughts might spark some interesting conversation.

By way of a tangible response or reaction to your reading this book, I would like to see the development of the book club phenomenon. Get a group together, read the book and beat the crap out of it. After you have given it a go going over, send me your ideas and revisions and I will incorporate your thoughts and ideas in the next edition!

See you down the road!

A Few Good Books

Block, P. (1993). *Stewardship: Choosing service over self-interest*. San Francisco, CA: Berrett-Koehler Publishers.

Bridges, W. (1994). *Job shift*. Reading, MA: Addison-Wesley Publishing Co.

Bunker, B.B. & Alban, B.T. (1997). *Large group interventions: Engaging the whole system for rapid change*. San Francisco, CA: Jossey-Bass Publishers.

Canadian Centre for Management Development, Deputy Ministers' Committee on Learning and Development, (2000). *Public service learning organization: From coast to coast to coast – directions for the future*.Ottawa, ON: Canadian Centre for Management Development.

Chawala, S. & Renensch, J. (eds.), (1995). *Learning organizations: Developing cultures for tomorrow's workplace*. Portland, OR: Productivity Press.

Florida, R. (2002). *The rise of the creative class*. New York, NY: Perseus.

Gladwell, M. (2000). *The tipping point: How little things can make a big difference*. New York, NY: Little, Brown & Co.

Goleman, D. (1998). *Working with emotional intelligence*. New York, NY: Bantam Books.

Goleman, D., Boyatzis, R. & McKee, A. (2002). *Primal leadership*. Boston, MA: Harvard Business School.

Hillman, J. (1996). *The soul's code*. New York, NY: Random House.

————. (1995). *Kinds of power*. New York, NY: Doubleday.

Hitchens, C. (2001). *Letters to a young contrarian*. Cambridge, MA: Perseus.

Homer-Dixon, T. (2001). *The ingenuity gap*. Toronto, ON: Vintage Canada.

Isaacs, W. (1999). *Dialogue and the art of thinking together.* New York, NY: Currency.

Klatt, B., Murphy, S. & Carter, W. (2001). *Accountability agreement workbook.* Calgary, AB: Murphy Klatt Consulting/Bow River Publishing.

Kleiner, A. (1996). *The age of heretics.* New York, NY: Doubleday.

Kouzes, J. M. & Posner, B.Z. (2002). *The leadership challenge.* San Francisco, CA: Jossey Bass Publishers.

Locke, C., Levine, R., Searls, D. & Weinburgr, D. (2000). *The cluetrain manifesto: The end of business as usual.* New York, NY: Perseus Publishing.

Osbourne, D. (1997). *Banishing bureaucracy.* New York, NY: Plume Publishing.

Osbourne, D. & Gaebler, T. (1992). *Reinventing government.* New York, NY: Plume Publishing.

Oshry, B. (1996). *Seeing systems.* San Francisco, CA: Berrett-Koehler Publishers.

Owen, H. (1992). *Open space technology: A user's guide.* Potomac, MD: Abbott Publishing.

Rilke, R. M. (1984). *Letters to a young poet.* New York, NY: Random House.

Schwartz, R. M. (1994). *The skilled facilitator.* San Francisco, CA: Jossey-Bass Inc.

Senge, P.M., (ed.), Cambron McCabe, N.H., Lucas, T., Kleiner, A., Dutton, J. & Smith, B. (2000). *Schools that learn: A fifth discipline fieldbook for educators, parents, and everyone who cares about education.* New York, NY: Doubleday.

Senge, P.M., Kleiner, A., Roberts, C., Roth, G., Ross, R. & Smith, B. (1999). *The dance of change: The challenges to sustaining momentum in learning organizations.* New York, NY: Doubleday.

Senge, P.M. & Kleiner, A. (eds.), Roberts, C., Ross, R. & Smith, B. (1994). *The fifth discipline fieldbook: Strategies and tools for building a learning organization.* New York, NY: Doubleday.

Senge, P.M. (1990). *The fifth discipline.* New York, NY: Doubleday.

Bureaucratically Incorrect

Terkel, S. (1972). *Working*. New York, NY: Random House.

Weisbord, M.R. (1992). *Discovering common ground*. San Francisco, CA: Berrett-Koehler Publishers.

———. (1991). *Productive workplaces: Organizing and managing for dignity, meaning and community*. San Francisco, CA: Jossey-Bass Publishers.

Welch, J. (2001). *Jack...straight from the gut*. New York: Warner Business Books.

Wenger, E., McDermott, R. & Snyder, W. M. (2002). *Cultivating communities of practice*. Boston, MA: Harvard Business School.

Wheatley, M. J. (1992). *Leadership and the new service: Learning about organization from an orderly universe*. San Francisco, CA: Berrett-Koehler.

Websites

Shaping a public service learning organization: From coast to coast to coast.
  <www.ccmd-ccg.gc.ca/learningtour/index.html>
The learning coach.
  <www.ccmd-ccg.gc.ca/learning-coach/webs/public/welcome.asp>
The leadership network.
  <www.leadership.gc.ca>
Coaching connection (at The Leadership Network website).
  <www.leadership.gc.ca/coaching>
The learning resource network.

Author Biography

OB Chartier has been a plumber, steelworker and a clumsy sawmill worker. He began a career in public service in education — first as a teacher, then a principal and finally as a superintendent of First Nations schools. During his tenure, Bob assisted with the transfer of more than fifty schools from federal to First Nations control. Bob also worked on a number of public participation projects including the groundbreaking Churchill River Study.

In mid career he returned to post graduate study at the University of Toronto with a focus on workplace learning. Afterwards, Bob returned to federal public service, working in partnership with the Department of Indian and Northern Affairs and The National Managers Community. He teleworks from his home in Calgary and spends much of his time crossing the country, working with public servants from all departments. His passion is in building learning organizations and promoting a leadership culture that recognizes leadership at all levels. His work has been recognized within government — with the Head of the Public Service Award in 2000 and in the private sector — with an invitation from Royal Roads University to be part of the faculty of the Personal Leadership in the Public Sector program.

As a former tradesman, Bob brings a practical, common sense approach to organizational change. He authored "Tools for Leadership and Learning" a utilitarian guide to building learning organizations. This guide is now promoted across the federal public service as a starting point for dialogue around building learning organization culture.

He identifies bad meetings, ubiquitous committees and self help workshops as prime targets for new tools. To that end Bob has pioneered the widespread use of such utilitarian tools as the Standup, the Workout,

Bureaucratically Incorrect

the Team Charter, OpenSpace and the Courtyard Café and has worked to modify these to fit the public sector.

Bob's specialties include facilitating large and small groups, conducting management seminars on practical, tool-based leadership and guest speaking. He uses humor, storytelling, and practical experience as the basis for his presentations. Leonard Cohen wrote a song in which he laments..."they sentenced me to twenty years of boredom, for trying to change the system from within..." Bob brings energy and enthusiasm to the world of organizational change as he continues to ask that old question, "Can you make change from the inside?" He remains convinced that we could and must do so.

As a continuous learner Bob spends his free time practicing the standup bass, honing his freelance writing skills and building furniture for his children and grandchildren.

A Call to Action

OB CHARTIER ENJOYS WORKING WITH public servants in all services and departments with whom he can explore how the principles and practices of a learning organization can transform the way they deliver their services to citizens.

He is a skilled facilitator and revels in the challenges inherent in taking a systems approach and getting everyone in the same room at the same time!

Bob is an accomplished seminar presenter and keynote speaker on topics such as leadership, change, teams, communication, and communities of practice and innovation.

You can reach him at:

#5 – 2318, 17th Street S.E.,
Calgary, Alberta
CANADA T2G 5R5
e-mail: chartb@telus.net
Phone: (403) 264•2919 / Fax: (403) 221•3079

2